LEADERS OF THE CIVIL WAR ERA

Jefferson Davis

LEADERS OF THE CIVIL WAR ERA

John Brown

Jefferson Davis

Frederick Douglass

Ulysses S. Grant

Stonewall Jackson

Robert E. Lee

Abraham Lincoln

William Tecumseh Sherman

Harriet Beecher Stowe

Harriet Tubman

LEADERS OF THE CIVIL WAR ERA

Jefferson Davis

David Aretha

CHELSEA HOUSE
PUBLISHERS

An imprint of Infobase Publishing

JEFFERSON DAVIS

Chelsea House
An imprint of Infobase Publishing
132 West 31st Street
New York NY 10001

Library of Congress Cataloging-in-Publication Data
Aretha, David.
  Jefferson Davis / David A. Aretha.
     p. cm. — (Leaders of the Civil War era)
  Includes bibliographical references and index.
  ISBN 978-1-60413-297-7 (hardcover)
  1. Davis, Jefferson, 1808-1889—Juvenile literature. 2. Presidents—Confederate States of America—Biography—Juvenile literature. I. Title. II. Series.
  E467.1.D26A74 2009
  973.7'13092—dc22
  [B]   2008044764

Chelsea House books are available at special discounts when purchased in bulk quantities for businesses, associations, institutions, or sales promotions. Please call our Special Sales Department in New York at (212) 967-8800 or (800) 322-8755.

You can find Chelsea House on the World Wide Web at http://www.chelseahouse.com

Series design by Erik Lindstrom
Cover design by Keith Trego

Printed in the United States of America

Bang FOF 10 9 8 7 6 5 4 3 2 1

This book is printed on acid-free paper.

All links and Web addresses were checked and verified to be correct at the time of publication. Because of the dynamic nature of the Web, some addresses and links may have changed since publication and may no longer be valid.

CONTENTS

"A Sentence of Death"

As daylight faded into darkness on February 10, 1861, a messenger hurriedly rode his horse through Natchez, Mississippi. He carried an urgent message to the Brierfield plantation, where dozens of slaves picked cotton for their master, Jefferson Davis.

Trimming stalks in the rose garden with his wife, Varina, Davis noticed the man on the galloping horse. The messenger greeted the slender, stately Davis and presented him with a telegram. Delegates of the new Confederate States of America, the message read, had elected Davis to be their new president. If the messenger expected a joyous reaction, he was sadly disappointed. When Davis told his wife the news, he looked, she wrote in her memoir, "as a man might speak of a sentence of death." Upon reading the telegram, he groaned, "Oh, God, spare me this responsibility."

Davis, 52 years old and of fragile health, had dreaded this very moment. He had nobly served the United States as a military commander in the Spanish-American War and later as the nation's secretary of war. Recently, he had resigned as U.S. senator from Mississippi following that state's secession from the Union. Mississippi and six other Southern states had all seceded after the antislavery Republican Party was elected to power in November 1860. The United States and the Confederacy were on the verge of civil war, Davis believed, and he was adverse to the position of president during such an ordeal.

Davis was more than willing to contribute, even as the commander of the Confederate armies, but not as president. He had deliberately avoided going to the Confederate convention in Montgomery, Alabama, but delegates elected him president anyway—unanimously. They could think of no finer representative to lead their fledgling nation. A man of great knowledge and character, Davis had delivered rousing speeches in the Senate and throughout the South. The delegates believed he would be a strong supporter of the seceded states without antagonizing the North with radical rhetoric. He could help the Confederacy achieve its goal: to remain a separate nation, with slavery and free trade, without interference from the North.

Out of allegiance to his new country, Davis accepted his election as provisional president. He hoped that the position would be temporary and that in time he could transfer to a position more suited to his liking. He would remain president, however, for the duration of the Confederacy.

After bidding sad farewells to Varina, their children, and his slaves—whom he had treated leniently—Davis set off for his inauguration in Montgomery. The South's railway system was so poor (at least in comparison to the North's) that it took Davis six days to reach his destination. Along the way, marching bands and excited citizens came out to greet him. In speech

On November 6, 1861, Jefferson Davis was elected to a six-year term as president of the Confederate States of America. As a U.S. senator from Mississippi he argued against secession, but had to back down when a majority of the delegates opposed him. When Mississippi seceded from the Union, Davis resigned from the Senate.

after speech, he declared that he wished to avoid war, but if conflict were inevitable, he would stand by the South "by shedding every drop of my blood in your cause."

The masses cheered such remarks, but Davis himself dreaded the thought of war. He knew that the Union boasted much greater resources, from manpower and industry to munitions and money. Still, he tried to bolster his country's morale. "It may be that our career will be ushered in amidst storm and trouble," he declared upon arriving in Montgomery. But, he added, "the progress of the Southern Confederacy will carry us safely over the sea of troubles."

On February 18, thousands lined Montgomery's Commerce Street on inauguration day. Cannons fired in celebration, and women tossed flowers at Davis as his carriage passed them by. During his inaugural address, Davis looked out upon a sea of smiling faces. His words of confidence delighted them all, but inside, Davis was a worried man. "The audience was large and brilliant," he later wrote to his wife. "Upon my weary heart was showered smiles, plaudits, and flowers...." But, he added ominously, "beyond them, I saw troubles and thorns innumerable."

Child of
the South

Nancy Hanks Lincoln and Jane Cook Davis did not know each other. Yet, in the spring of 1808, they shared much in common. Each woman lived in a log cabin in Kentucky and each was pregnant with a future president. Nancy's son, Abraham, would rise to the presidency of the United States in March 1861, while Jane's would become leader of the Confederate States of America two weeks earlier.

Entering the world on June 3, 1808, Jane's baby was named Jefferson Finis Davis. His first and middle names carried significant meaning. Jane and her husband, Samuel, named their son after the reigning president, Thomas Jefferson. The president lauded the men and women who worked the land, such as Samuel and Jane and, one day, Jefferson himself. President Jefferson was also a Southerner and a firm supporter of states' rights, which Davis would champion throughout his political career.

Young Jefferson's middle name, Finis, means "final" in Latin. Samuel, who was known for his wit, may have chosen this name because this was to be their final child. Jane had already borne nine children, and she was 46 years old. He was over 50. But *finis*, in association with Davis, would in time have poetic meaning: the end of the Old South.

Davis was descended from old soldiers. His mother's uncle was Nathaniel Greene, a famous Revolutionary War general. Davis's father had also served in the American Revolution, fighting as a captain in Georgia. According to Davis, as noted in *The Iron Will of Jefferson Davis,* his father was "unusually handsome . . . an accomplished horseman . . . usually grave and stoical . . . and of such sound judgment that his opinions were law to his children." Davis would grow up to be much like his father.

A HAPPY CHILDHOOD

When Jefferson was two, his father moved his family from Kentucky down south to the Louisiana Territory. President Thomas Jefferson had acquired this vast amount of land—which comprised the central third of the present United States—from the French in 1803. It coincided with the spirit of Manifest Destiny, Americans' belief that the United States was destined to expand from the Atlantic coast all the way to the Pacific. This dream would become reality in the first half of the 1800s, but with it came debates over slavery. Should new, western states be added as free states or slave states? This was a question that Jefferson Davis would address as a political figure.

As a young boy, though, he was more concerned about mosquitoes. The Davis family found fertile land to farm in Louisiana, but the bugs in the area carried malaria. Unwilling to endure the insects, the Davises moved to southwestern Mississippi for a more traditional Southern life. Samuel, his

One of the most divisive issues in American history has been the concept of Manifest Destiny (depicted in the painting *Across the Continent* above). Manifest Destiny was the idea that it was the God-given right of the United States to take over all of North America, from the Atlantic to the Pacific. In 1848, Senator Jefferson Davis, a supporter of expansionism, declared "Cuba must be ours" in order to "increase the number of slaveholding constituencies."

sons, and a few slaves cleared land and planted cotton and other crops. They also built a cottage on land that was surrounded by poplar trees. Jane planted rose gardens, prompting the family to call their home Rosemont.

By all accounts, Jefferson enjoyed his childhood. He had loving parents and plenty of siblings who liked to play with their baby brother. Jefferson and his sister Polly, just two years older than him, played in the poplar groves and picked fruit in the orchard. He also learned how to fish, ride horses, and shoot a gun.

At first, Jefferson attended school in a log cabin about a mile from home, but at age eight his life changed dramatically.

Samuel wanted Jefferson to develop into a noble Southern gentleman and that meant he would need to attain the finest education. With no good schools in the area, Samuel decided to send him to a Catholic school in Kentucky called the College of St. Thomas Aquinas. Jane strongly opposed the idea, but she could not dissuade her husband.

OFF TO SCHOOL

In 1816, Jefferson began his first great adventure. He left for Kentucky with Major Thomas Hinds (a friend of his brother Joseph) and his family. Stopping in Nashville, Jefferson and the Hinds family visited General Andrew Jackson, the hero of the War of 1812. The visit went so well, in fact, that they wound up staying for several weeks. Jefferson found the old warrior to be kind and courteous, and he always said grace before meals. Little did anyone know that Jackson would, in 1829, become president of the United States.

The College of St. Thomas Aquinas was not a college but rather a preparatory school for boys. The first such Catholic school west of the Allegheny Mountains, it boasted an enrollment of some 200 students. Jefferson, one of the youngest kids in the school, shared a room with an old priest. He received a first-class education, especially in foreign languages, but he stayed at the school for only two years. In 1818, the Wilkinson County Academy—the first good school near Rosemont—opened its doors. Samuel decided to enroll his youngest child there. Riding a steamboat down the Mississippi River that year, Davis returned home. His mother and even his stoic father welcomed him with hugs and kisses.

Jefferson spent five years at Wilkinson, but he was not particularly attentive. One day, after being reprimanded by a teacher for not mastering his subject matter, Davis grabbed his books and went home. His father gave him a choice. "I want more cotton-pickers," he told his son, as documented in *The Papers of Jefferson Davis*, "and will give you work." For two days, he toiled in the cotton fields with slaves and other laborers. Was this how he wanted to spend his life? Jefferson thought not, and he returned to school.

Samuel knew how hard it was to earn a living. In 1822, he was forced to sell Rosemont to his oldest son, Joseph, a prosperous attorney and landowner. Jefferson's education, however, would not be sacrificed. In 1823, he was enrolled at Transylvania University in Kentucky, where many Southern aristocrats sent their sons. There, Davis would develop exceptional skills in debating—a key factor in his future political career. However, before his first school year ended, Jefferson received horrible news from home: His father had suffered from fever, and he had died on the Fourth of July 1824. His last piece of advice for his youngest son was contained in a letter: "Use every possible means to acquire useful knowledge as knowledge is power."

A REBELLIOUS CADET

Before Samuel died, he and Joseph agreed that Jefferson should go to the U.S. Military Academy in West Point, New York. Jefferson argued about this with his older brother, saying he wanted to be a lawyer, not a military man. They eventually agreed that he would go to the academy for one year and then transfer to the University of Virginia if he wanted to.

Because of the martial tradition in the South, most of the cadets at West Point were Southerners. In fact, Davis would come to rely on many of these cadets when he became president of the Confederacy. West Point's Robert E. Lee, Albert Sidney Johnston, Joseph E. Johnston, and John Magruder would all serve as Confederate generals during the Civil War.

As for Davis, he did not seem cut out for military life. Showing disdain for the academy's rigid rules, he committed numerous infractions. He disobeyed orders, skipped drills, dressed inappropriately, and even fired his rifle out his window. Davis hung out with fellow rebels and was nearly expelled.

VIEW OF THE U. S. MILITARY ACADEMY AND THE NEW BARRACKS, AT WEST POINT, N. Y.

Davis was appointed to West Point through his brother Joseph's political connections from the office of Secretary of State John C. Calhoun. Davis attended the academy with many notable men that would later play a major part in the Civil War. He graduated twenty-third in a class of 32.

Once, while returning from the Benny Havens tavern (which was supposed to be off-limits for cadets), Davis fell 60 feet down a riverbank. His injuries landed him in the hospital for four months.

After four years, Davis graduated from West Point in 1828. He ranked twenty-third in a class of 32. In his final year, he had amassed 137 demerits! Despite his misadventures, it had been a worthwhile four years. He respected the academy, had forged strong friendships, and had developed a keen interest in military science. He also impressed his fellow cadets, with one quoted in *The Life of Jefferson Davis*: "Jefferson Davis was distinguished in the corps for his manly bearing, his high-toned and lofty character. His figure was very soldier-like and rather robust; his step springy, resembling the tread of an Indian 'brave' on the war-path."

In July 1828, he was ready to serve in the U.S. Army—at least for a few years. Davis was appointed brevet second lieutenant, and he received orders to report to the Infantry School of Practice at Jefferson Barracks in Missouri. His service wouldn't begin until October 30. Until then, he was allowed to spend time with his family in Mississippi. Davis welcomed the opportunity for he had not seen his family in more than five years.

Love and Sorrow

The Rosemont that Davis remembered was not the same when he returned there in 1828. Only his mother, his sister Lucinda, and Lucinda's three daughters lived at the house. Davis visited his brother Isaac, who had become disabled after a cyclone blasted his house (and killed his son). Davis also reunited with a slave named James Pemberton. Davis's father, Samuel, had designated Pemberton as Davis's personal servant. When the young lieutenant left for Missouri in October 1828 to report for duty, Pemberton went with him.

Shortly after arriving in Missouri, Davis was transferred to Fort Crawford in what would, in a few years, become Wisconsin Territory. His mission was to oversee a crew that would repair and enlarge the old fort. To do so, they needed lumber, but unfortunately the area was virtually treeless. Davis knew little about building forts, but he rose to the occasion. He and his men paddled canoes up to a northern forest some 175 miles away. Twice the men avoided attacks by hostile American Indians, and eventually they produced enough lumber for their fort, which they pulled in rafts down the river.

Late in 1829, Davis was reassigned to Fort Winnebago in east-central Wisconsin. At the time, only the hardiest of pioneers lived in this frigid, undeveloped region. Davis admired the brave souls who built cabins, cleared land, and raised crops with their own hands and simple tools. American Indians were known to set cabins on fire and kidnap children. Yet, Davis also admired them: the Winnebago, Sioux, Comanche, and other tribes. They could fish with just spears, and American Indian mail runners carried heavy bags of letters 40 miles a day.

The white families also knew how to have fun: card games, theatricals, sleigh rides, and dances. Davis, who had learned proper dancing techniques at West Point, became popular with the ladies at such events. He also enjoyed reading and riding wild horses, but life in Wisconsin was not all fun and games. At times, Davis and his fellow soldiers left to fend off hostile tribes. In one instance, he rode up to an American Indian whom he believed had lied to him. Davis grabbed him by the hair and dragged him before violently releasing him.

Yet in 1831, after being recalled to Fort Crawford and then sent to construct a sawmill, Davis worked to make friends with American Indians. They returned the favor, calling him "Little Chief." The sawmill project actually gave him more trouble than the natives. Snow fell relentlessly that winter, but Davis and his crew tried to work through it. The Southerner caught a virus and did not have the resistance to fight it off. He lost weight, became nearly delirious, and reached a point where he could not walk. Davis trusted his slave, James Pemberton, with his money and weapons, and his faithful servant did what he could to help him convalesce. At times, he carried his master

During its second occupation, Fort Crawford, in present-day Prairie du Chien, Wisconsin, was used from 1832-1856 as a military garrison along the upper Mississippi River. Davis served as lieutenant at the fort under Colonel Zachary Taylor.

to the window to see the glistening snow. Davis recovered, but he would battle illnesses the rest of his life.

Upon his return to Fort Crawford to oversee the enlargement of the fort, Davis's adventures continued. When one muscle-bound soldier declared that he would not take orders from the boyish-looking lieutenant, Davis knocked him down with a piece of wood. From then on, few dared to question his authority.

LOSING SARAH

While at Fort Crawford, Davis began courting Sarah Knox Taylor, the daughter of the fort's commander. Colonel Zachary

Taylor, in fact, would go on to become president of the United States—just like Andrew Jackson, whom Davis had known as a child. In the spring of 1833, Davis asked the colonel if he could marry his daughter. Taylor said no, claiming that he did not want any of his three daughters marrying a military man. Soldiers were gone too much, Colonel Taylor reasoned, and their lives were often in jeopardy.

Davis was head over heals for Sarah, however. According to relatives, the eighteen-year-old woman was, as told in *Jefferson Davis: An American Patriot*, "very beautiful, slight, with wavy brown hair and clear gray eyes, very lovely and lovable, and a young woman of the decided spirit." Davis went home and discussed the matter with his oldest brother. Joseph offered him 800 acres of land and a loan to buy slaves, who would pick cotton. That sounded good to Davis. He submitted his letter of resignation to the War Department, and on June 17, 1835, he married Sarah. The wedding was held in Louisville, Kentucky, at the home of Zachary Taylor's sister.

Tragically, Davis's bliss would soon spiral into immense sorrow. Married life started well, as the couple lived in Joseph's large house while Jefferson oversaw the clearing of land that Joseph had given him. Because the land was overrun with briers, Jefferson called the plantation Brierfield. Sarah's mother worried about disease-carrying mosquitoes during the hot, humid summer, as did Jefferson. He took his wife to a safer area, at his sister's home in Louisiana, but by the time they got there, they were already stricken with malaria. One night, while they both lay ill at his sister's place, Sarah began singing a song they loved, "Fairy Bells." It was her last waking moment, for she soon slipped into unconsciousness. On September 15, three months after their wedding, she died.

ALONE WITH HIS BOOKS

Ravaged by grief and illness, Davis hovered near death for days. In mid-October, his servant James carried him to a boat, which he took to Joseph's plantation. Davis recovered his health but not his spirit. Forever after, he remained serious and stoic—a rock who was unwilling to express his emotions.

Once healthy enough to travel, Davis convalesced in Cuba for a while. He then spent time in Washington, D.C., where he attended congressional sessions. At the time, white settlers in the Mexican Republic of Texas were revolting against the Mexican government. In 1836, the rebels would prevail and form the Republic of Texas. Davis heard the pleas of Southerners who wanted to admit the enormous territory as

HOW WERE SLAVES TREATED?

Not all punishment inflicted on slaves was physical. Slave owners exerted total control over the lives of these men and women and took away their most basic rights. One former slave, John Andrew Jackson, recalled in *The Experience of a Slave in South Carolina*:

> I fell in love with a slave girl named Louisa, who belonged to a Mrs. Wells, whose plantation was about a mile off.... Shortly after, I married Louisa. Do not let the reader run away with the idea that there was any marriage ceremony, for the poor slaves are debarred that privilege by the cruel hand of their fellow-man. My master was exceedingly angry when he heard of my marriage, because my children would not belong to him, and whenever he discovered that I had visited my wife's plantation during the night, I was tied up and received fifty lashes. But no man can be prevented from visiting his wife, and the consequence was, that I was beaten on the average, at least every week for that offense. I shall carry these

a state—a *slave* state. But many Northerners, those opposed to slavery, objected. Such weighty matters would consume Davis in the upcoming years.

From 1836 to 1843, Davis lived a quiet life on his Brierfield plantation. With the manpower of more than a dozen slaves, he built a house, planted trees, cleared his land, and planted cotton. Brierfield was so close to the Mississippi River that during the rainy season the river would sometimes flood the cotton fields. Otherwise, the slaves picked cotton for their master so that he could enjoy a comfortable life.

scars to my grave. My wife had two children, one of whom died. But we were soon separated, as her owner removed to Georgia, and we were parted forever.

Not all slaveholders treated their chattel as badly. Susan Dabney Smedes, in *Memorials of a Southern Planter*, recalled how her father dealt with his slaves.

His plantation was considered a model one and was visited by planters anxious to learn his methods. He was asked how he made his Negroes do good work. His answer was that a laboring man could do more work and better work in five and a half days than in six... He distributed prizes of money among his cotton pickers every week during the season, which lasted four or five months.

Northern abolitionists would have condemned both men. They believed that no people, no matter their race or how well they were treated, should be possessed by others.

Davis believed that the institution of slavery was sanctioned by the Bible and black labor was necessary in order to develop the cotton trade in the South, which Southerners depended on for their livelihood. At the same time, he believed that gradual emancipation would come to the slave, and he allowed them to hold their own courts and set their own punishments. Pictured here are the slave quarters on Rosemont Plantation, Davis' boyhood home.

Davis believed in white supremacy and strongly supported slavery. He also saw the need for local militias that maintained order among slaves and hunted down runaway slaves. Yet Davis was also a benevolent slave owner, refusing to whip or physically abuse his servants. Relatively speaking, he treated them well, and he trusted them so much that he allowed them to use his guns to go hunting. Davis continued to purchase slaves, and by 1840 he owned 40.

Davis spent much of his ample free time reading books and newspapers. He scoured books about history, law, economics, political philosophy, and the military. He also kept abreast of the politics of the day. Among the hot topics were the Northern abolitionists, who railed against the inhumanity of slavery. Southerners portrayed the abolitionists as fanatics who were out to destroy the Southern way of life. Without slaves, Southerners insisted, plantation owners would go out of business. They would not be able to afford to pay laborers.

The North and South also argued about tariffs—taxes on imports. In the 1830s, the United States had high tariffs on manufactured goods. This raised the price of imported goods and, thus, allowed Northern manufacturers to charge high prices for their products. The South, being mostly an agricultural region, did not benefit from high tariffs. In fact, it suffered because its citizens had to pay artificially high prices for the goods produced in Northern factories. Southern politicians were so irate about this issue that they sometimes talked about seceding from the United States.

In retrospect, it would not have been surprising if Davis had never left the comforts of Brierfield. The death of his wife had made him quiet and reclusive, and he had never seemed to have great ambition. Still, the more familiar he became with the issues of the day, the more restless he got. In 1843, at the age of 34, Davis was ready to delve into a new career: politics.

Congressman and War Hero

Before delving into politics, Davis had to decide which party to enter. Most of his fellow Southern aristocrats belonged to the Whig Party. The Democrats were the "party of the people," representing the many laborers and farmers who toiled throughout the South. The Democrats espoused the values of President Thomas Jefferson, after whom Davis was named. Davis decided to join the Democrats.

Davis attended state Democratic meetings, and in 1843, he decided to run for a seat in Mississippi's House of Representatives. He lost the election, but he displayed remarkable insight into state and national politics. Moreover, his eloquent orations on behalf of states' rights won over Democratic Party leaders. In fact, he was chosen to be one of Mississippi's electors for James Polk, who would run for the presidency against the Whig Party's Henry Clay in 1844.

For months leading up to the November 1844 election, Davis toured Mississippi on horses, steamboats, stagecoaches, and carriages. Wherever he went, he spoke on behalf of Polk and the party. In the memoir of Varina Davis (his second wife), an acquaintance named Reuben Davis describes Jefferson Davis as "[d]ignified and commanding, soft and persuasive, his speech was from beginning to end a finished piece of logic and oratory."

Jefferson Davis voiced his approval of aggressive foreign policy. He believed the United States should annex the Republic of Texas, even though such a move would likely start a war with Mexico. He also supported annexing part of the Oregon Territory, which the British claimed was theirs. In addition, he backed low tariffs and the strengthening of states' rights.

DAVIS REMARRIES

Nine years after the death of his wife, Sarah, Davis was embracing life again. He even met a young woman, 17-year-old Varina Banks Howell, with whom he quickly fell in love. The daughter of his brother Joseph's friend, Varina was well educated and exceptionally intelligent. Her initial opinion of Davis was dead on. She wrote to her mother, "He impresses me as a remarkable kind of man, but of uncertain temper, and has a way of taking for granted that everybody agrees with him when he expresses an opinion." Varina did agree with him when he asked for her hand in marriage. On February 26, 1845, they exchanged vows at her parents' home.

Davis's star was on the rise in 1845. After enjoying a six-week honeymoon, he was nominated by the state Democratic Party for a seat in the U.S. House of Representatives. That November, he won. Just two years after entering politics, he was now a United States congressman. As he and Varina prepared to move to Washington, Davis trained James Pemberton to oversee Brierfield. His most trusted slave would oversee the other slaves, who now numbered more than 70.

When Varina Howell met Jefferson Davis at the age of 17, her parents did not think they were a good match and were against their engagement. Davis was widowed, moody, and much older than Varina. Eventually, her parents relented and the couple married on February 26, 1845.

Just days after taking office, Davis wowed Congress with his orations. During one speech, he called for the annexation of part of the Oregon Territory (which extended way north to Alaska) but not all of it. Democratic expansionists wanted the entire territory, but such a bold takeover would undoubtedly

VARINA HOWELL DAVIS

Following the death of his first wife, Sarah, in 1835, Davis lived in seclusion at his Brierfield plantation. But in 1843, he met 17-year-old Varina Banks Howell at a Christmas party. He was immediately attracted by her beauty, intelligence, and charm.

Varina was an excellent match for the wealthy plantation owner turned politician, 18 years her senior. She moved with him to Washington, D.C., upon his appointment to the U.S. Senate. She loved the bustling social life in the nation's capital, and the Davis family remained there until the threat of war forced them to return to the South.

After being elected president of the Confederate States of America, Davis established his government in Richmond, Virginia. In the White House of the Confederacy, Varina made a home for her family.

The first lady of the Confederacy was a close confidante of her husband. In fact, many of the other politicians' wives were jealous of Varina's intellect and position in the new government. Behind her back, many referred to her as Queen Varina. Although doubting the ultimate success of the war, she worked hard to support Confederate soldiers and their families through donations of food and clothing.

After the Civil War and two years of imprisonment for treason, Davis failed at a number of business ventures. Varina helped to support the family as a part-time seamstress. Following her husband's death in 1889, she moved to New York, a world away from her roots at Natchez.

trigger war with Great Britain. Under President Polk's command in the spring of 1846, the United States and Great Britain did indeed agree on a compromise. The United States took claim of the southern section of the territory, leaving the northern part for Great Britain. Thus, war was averted.

When it came to the issue of Mexico, however, Davis had no qualms about going to war. Tensions between the two nations came to a head in 1845, when the U.S. Congress approved the Republic of Texas's request to join the United States. Mexico, which still considered Texas its possession, severed diplomatic relations with the United States. Mexican officials also did not recognize the Rio Grande as Texas's southern boundary, and Mexican troops showed their defiance by crossing it repeatedly. After diplomatic attempts failed, U.S. president James Polk ordered General Zachary Taylor's troops to the Rio Grande to establish the border.

THE HERO OF BUENA VISTA

On May 11, 1846, Congress declared war on Mexico—a decision strongly supported by Davis. When President Polk asked the states to organize volunteer regiments to support the undersized U.S. Army, Davis stated that he himself should lead the Mississippi volunteers. Against Varina's wishes, he was elected colonel and commander of the 1st Mississippi Infantry Regiment. In July, Davis and 900 volunteers sailed to the Rio Grande. Once in Texas, they trained with the new Whitney rifles, which Davis had purchased with his own money. The regiment became known as the Mississippi Rifles.

Soon, Davis's troops joined forces with those of General Taylor, his former father-in-law. Together, they defeated Mexican forces at Monterrey. The big battle, however, occurred at Buena Vista in northern Mexico in February 1847. President Polk, feeling threatened by Taylor's growing popularity, reassigned many of his troops to the battlefront in Mexico City. Learning about Taylor's vulnerability, Mexican general Santa

In June 1846, Davis resigned from the House of Representatives to fight in the Mexican-American War. In recognition of his bravery, his former father-in-law, General Zachary Taylor, is reputed to have said, "My daughter, sir, was a better judge of men than I was." In this painting, General Taylor (on the white horse) directs his men during the Battle of Buena Vista in 1847.

Anna sent a large army to Buena Vista. Outnumbering the Americans four to one, the Mexicans began to overpower the U.S. forces. Davis himself was shot in the foot.

But when Taylor ordered Davis's men to attempt a desperate charge at the enemy, they responded with valor. Attacking in a wedge formation (a stroke of brilliance by Davis), the U.S. troops ended the Mexican advance. America won the battle, and Davis was hailed as the "hero of Buena Vista." Taylor would ride the victory all the way to the White House, winning the election in 1848 after Polk decided not to run.

SENATOR DURING TURBULENT TIMES

With their one-year enlistment over, the Mississippi Rifles—including Davis, on crutches—went home in June 1847. By early 1848, the United States had won the Mexican-American War. The United States took not only Texas but the future states of California, Nevada, and Utah, as well as parts of what would become Colorado, Arizona, New Mexico, and Wyoming. The victory thrilled Americans, but it also opened a political can of worms.

Up to that point, Congress had maintained a delicate balance of free states and slave states. Too many free states would greatly upset the South and vice versa. In fact, if three-quarters of the states were free, they would have the congressional power to amend the U.S. Constitution and abolish slavery. Such a scenario would devastate the South's economy. So what would happen when new territories in the Southwest (and Northwest) applied for statehood? To which side, slave or free, would the scale tip? This question would consume politicians for years to come.

When Mississippi legislators needed to fill a U.S. Senate seat in December 1847, they did not have to think long. Unanimously, they selected war hero and master orator Jefferson Davis. The following year, the people of Mississippi elected him to a six-year term. Davis strongly supported states' rights and the practice of slavery. In fact, he even put forth an amendment to the U.S. Constitution that would prevent Congress from prohibiting slavery. The amendment did not pass, but Davis's conviction remained strong. During one speech, he declared that if the North ignored the will of the South, "We should part peaceably, and avoid staining the battlefields of the Revolution with the blood of civil war."

Due to the gold rush in California in the late 1840s, tens of thousands of people poured into that territory. By 1850, it was ready to become a state. But would it be a slave state or free? At the time, half of the 30 states were slave and the other half were free. Senator Henry Clay proposed the Compromise of

1850. According to the bill, California would be a free state but other newly acquired southwest territories would decide the slavery question through their legislatures. The South would be rewarded with the Fugitive Slave Act, which was designed to force Northern states to return fugitive slaves.

Davis and aged senator John Calhoun of South Carolina led the fight to defeat the compromise. Davis argued that the rights of the Southern states were not being adequately protected. Nonetheless, more moderate Southern congressmen—fearing a divided Union and perhaps a civil war—supported the compromise. In September 1850, the bill passed.

In 1851, Democratic Party leaders in Mississippi asked Davis to run for governor. He obliged, resigning from Congress to do so. Davis ran against Whig candidate Henry S. Foote, who had supported the compromise. At the time, Southerners feared secession, and Davis felt compelled to declare that he opposed such an extreme action. Nevertheless, he lost to Foote by a narrow margin. Frustrated by the defeat, Davis returned to Brierfield.

Davis's wife, Varina, was glad to have him home. Not only was the plantation in disarray, but she was pregnant. At age 43, Davis was about to become a father for the first time.

Spokesman
for the South

Early in 1852, Davis enjoyed his respite from politics. After four years, he and his slaves finally completed a larger house on the Brierfield plantation. Each day, Jefferson and Varina went horseback riding—sometimes on forest roads. They delighted in the scents of cedar trees and sage, plum blossom, and sassafras. Davis frequently greeted and praised his slaves, who seemed to have genuine affection for their master.

On July 30, 1852, Varina gave birth to the couple's first child, Samuel, who they named after Davis's father. The Davises gave the slaves a day off, and they came to the house bearing such gifts as wildflowers, fruit, and yams. While overjoyed by the birth of his son, Davis was outraged by a new book that was taking the nation by storm. Harriet Beecher Stowe's *Uncle Tom's Cabin*, which would become the biggest-selling novel

UNCLE TOM'S
=CABIN=

A GREAT WRONG RIGHTED.

The anti-slavery novel *Uncle Tom's Cabin* by Harriet Beecher Stowe had a profound effect on America's attitude toward slavery in the United States. The book was a best-seller, and it ignited a storm of protest from defenders of slavery, while also eliciting praise from abolitionists. It is said to be responsible for making an already tense situation between the North and South even worse.

of the nineteenth century, focused on the horrors of slavery and the cruelty of Southern slave owners. The book inspired Northerners to lash out against the "Southern way."

Southerners retorted that slaveholders did not treat their slaves as badly as Stowe had claimed. Davis had graver concerns. He feared that the book would disturb the fragile peace that existed between the North and South. His concern was justified. After the Civil War began, according to legend, President Abraham Lincoln said to Stowe, "So this is the little lady who made this big war."

DAVIS SHINES AS SECRETARY OF WAR

Davis did not leave politics altogether in 1852. He contributed to the presidential campaign of Franklin Pierce, his old friend from the Mexican-American War. After Pierce defeated Whig candidate Winfield Scott, he offered Davis a position in his cabinet. Davis would be the nation's secretary of war.

It may seem ironic that the main enemy of the United States in the 1860s oversaw its military in the 1850s. Yet in his four years as secretary of war, Davis proved to be devoted, productive, and innovative. In fact, historians rate him among the best secretaries of war and defense in American history. Davis helped increase the size of the U.S. Army and improve the pay for soldiers. He modernized the military's weapons and instilled new training tactics. He also helped establish a medical corps.

Through much of the nineteenth century, the federal government tried to protect western settlers from American Indian attacks. Davis established strategically placed forts and created mobile cavalry units to go after hostile American Indians. In 1855, to help the army in the Southwest, Davis imported 74 camels from North Africa. Davis believed that these desert beasts would provide superior service as army pack animals as they traveled the vast distances of the arid Southwest. The camel experiment proved successful and continued up until the Civil War.

Davis wielded exceptional power as secretary of war. He oversaw the mapping of a route for a transcontinental railroad. The coast-to-coast railroad, completed in 1869, would allow people and goods to travel westward easily and quickly. Davis's good friend President Franklin Pierce often listened to his advice on political matters. Not surprisingly, Davis advocated policies that would strengthen the South. He urged President Pierce to expand the American empire to Cuba and Nicaragua, which would make them slave territories. Such efforts never came to fruition, however.

In June 1854, tragedy struck the Davis family. Early in the month, his young son, Samuel, contracted a disease. Doctors could not determine the cause of the illness, and the boy's health increasingly declined. On June 30, he died. Hundreds of people offered their sympathies, but Davis could not come to grips with the loss. Varina wrote that for weeks afterward, "he walked half the night, and worked fiercely all day." Davis presented a stoic façade, but according to Varina, the sound of a crying baby would make him distressed.

In subsequent years, Varina would bear five more children. Their daughters Margaret and Varina Anne would grow into adulthood, but it seemed that fate would prevent Davis from having a male heir. All three of their other sons failed to live past the age of 21.

BLEEDING KANSAS

In the mid-1850s, the slavery issue rose to the fore. In the former Louisiana Territory, slavery had not been permitted north of 36°30' (Missouri's southern boundary). But by 1854, most Northerners and Southerners no longer wanted an artificial boundary to determine the status of future states. That year, U.S. senator Stephen A. Douglas of Illinois proposed that a

Pro-slavery activists, also known as Border Ruffians, were encouraged to defend the institution of slavery with violence, if necessary. The Kansas-Nebraska Act left open to elections the question of whether Kansas Territory would be a slave or free state. Bands of Border Ruffians poured into Kansas Territory from the neighboring slave state of Missouri. They intimidated voters and battled free-state forces, who also committed atrocities against settlers who did not support their cause.

territory's people, just prior to statehood, should vote whether they wanted slavery in their state. "Popular sovereignty," it was called. After congressmen furiously debated this proposal, it passed as part of the Kansas-Nebraska Act of 1854.

The new law led to disaster. Large amounts of pro-slavery supporters from the South moved to Kansas Territory, most notably to Missouri, to secure the expansion of slavery. At the same time, free-soilers (abolitionists) funded several thousand settlers to move to Kansas to make sure it became a free state.

In November 1854, thousands of armed Southerners, known as Border Ruffians, poured into Kansas from Missouri in an attempt to influence the vote on making Kansas a slave or free state. By the summer of 1855, an estimated 1,200 New Englanders had made the journey, armed and ready to fight.

The territory became a battleground in 1856 and 1857, as heavily armed proslavery and antislavery proponents fought each other on the plains. On May 21, 1856, a group of Border Ruffians burned the Free State Hotel in Lawrence, Kansas, destroyed two newspaper offices, and ransacked homes and stores. The day after, Senator Charles Sumner of Massachusetts was severely beaten with his own cane by Congressman Preston Brooks from South Carolina in the Senate chambers. Sumner had criticized Southerners for proslavery violence in Kansas. He did not return to his Senate desk for three years due to his injuries. In retaliation for violence by Border Ruffians, fanatical abolitionist John Brown and a group of men went to the Kansas Territory to attack a proslavery settlement. They led seven men from their homes and stabbed them to death with broadswords. As secretary of war, Davis sent in federal troops to stop Kansas from "bleeding." They succeeded in stemming most of the violence, but tensions remained at a fever-pitch.

JOINING A DIVIDED SENATE

In 1856, during his fourth year as secretary of war, Davis was ready for a new challenge. Many said he would make a fine vice presidential candidate, but Davis was not interested in the position. Instead, he wanted to return to the U.S. Senate. He ran for an open Senate seat, and Mississippians voted him in. It would be the last post he would hold in the federal government.

Meanwhile, the political winds were changing in Washington. Democrats did not nominate incumbent president Franklin Pierce, largely because he had supported the disastrous Kansas-Nebraska Act. Instead they nominated former secretary of state James Buchanan. His opponent was John Frémont of the new

Republican Party, which strongly opposed slavery. Fearing that a Republican victory would cause Southern states to secede from the Union and trigger a civil war, American voters elected Buchanan—although Frémont carried 11 of the 31 states.

KING COTTON

In a speech before the U.S. Senate on March 4, 1858, Senator James Henry Hammond of South Carolina declared,

> [W]ould any sane nation make war on cotton? Without firing a gun, without drawing a sword, should they make war on us we could bring the whole world to our feet.... England would topple headlong and carry the whole civilized world with her, save the South. No, you dare not make war on cotton. No power on earth dares to make war upon it. Cotton is king. Until lately the Bank of England was king; but she tried to put her screws as usual, the fall before last, upon the cotton crop, and was utterly vanquished. The last power has been conquered.

Hammond had every reason to believe that cotton held an important position in the world's economy. After Eli Whitney's invention of the cotton gin, Southern cotton exports increased from 140,000 pounds in 1792 to more than 64 million pounds by 1811. In the early 1800s, the South produced more than 60 percent of the world's cotton supply, which bolstered the rise of the textile industry in England and New England.

At the outset of the Civil War, Southerners believed that England would intervene on the South's behalf to maintain its cotton imports. But when the supply of cotton from America stopped, England turned to other countries for its needs. King Cotton, not England, was vanquished.

Davis immersed himself in slavery issues. For months he toured Mississippi, appearing at social gatherings and talking to everyday people—not just plantation owners, but individual farmers and those of other occupations. While strongly defending slavery in his speeches (and labeling Northerners as agitators), he also asked what the people thought. Would they be willing to secede from the Union in defense of slavery, even though most did not own slaves themselves? Would they go to war to preserve the Southern way of life?

Davis acknowledged that the South was too reliant on cotton and slave labor, that it needed to modernize and diversify its industries. Still, he was so supportive of the institution of slavery that he favored the idea of importing more slaves from Africa. He reasoned that the South needed the extra manpower in order to prosper. The U.S. government had banned the importing of slaves in 1808, but Davis felt that states should be able to make their own decisions on the matter.

THE LEADING VOICE OF THE SOUTH

In March 1857, the month that Davis was sworn in as a U.S. senator, the Supreme Court announced its historic *Dred Scott* decision. The case was based on a slave, Dred Scott, who had traveled with his master, Dr. John Emerson, to Illinois and Fort Snelling in the Illinois Territory. Both of these places were free states. After living there for an extended period of time, Scott and his new wife (who thought they were free since they had lived in free states) traveled south to meet with his master, who eventually died in 1843. Scott was hired out to an army captain by Emerson's widow, and Scott offered to buy his and his wife's freedom, but the offer was refused. Scott then sought freedom through the courts. The Supreme Court ruled seven to two against Scott, stating that no person of African ancestry could claim citizenship in the United States, therefore Scott could not bring suit in federal court. In addition, Scott's temporary residence outside Missouri did not effect his emancipation under the Missouri Compromise, and the federal government could not revoke a slave owner's right to own a slave based on where he lived. Slavery advocates celebrated the news, while abolitionists were outraged.

For the next four years, politicians on both sides of the issue delivered thunderous speeches about slavery and states' rights. Republican senator William Seward proclaimed that when it came to slavery, Americans should follow not federal law but a "higher law"—God's law. Declared Seward in a speech, "And now the simple, bold, and even awful question which presents itself to us is this. . . . Shall we establish human bondage, or permit it by our sufferance to be established? . . . I confess that the most alarming evidence of our degeneracy . . . is found in that we even debate such a question."

Davis was outraged by the notion that Americans should follow their conscience and not the law of the United States government. As senator, he became an even more ardent defender of slavery and states' rights. And when he spoke, people listened. Famed editor Horace Greeley of the *New York Tribune* described Davis as "unquestionably the foremost man of the South today. Every Northern Senator will admit that from the Southern side of the floor the most formidable to meet in debate is the thin, polished, intellectual-looking Mississippian with the unimpassioned demeanor. . . ."

Extremists on both sides of the slave debate called for punitive measures. Abolitionists declared that the North should become less dependent on Southern, slave-picked cotton. Conversely, Southerners urged their businessmen to find foreign markets, instead of Northern, for their cotton. But Southerners would not find much foreign sympathy for their practice of slavery. Great Britain, for one, had outlawed slavery throughout its empire back in 1833.

The stress of the times caught up to Davis. Early in 1858, he caught a bad cold and severe laryngitis. Nerve spasms paralyzed one side of his face, and his left eye became inflamed. The eye pain was so bad that he could not bear the slightest light.

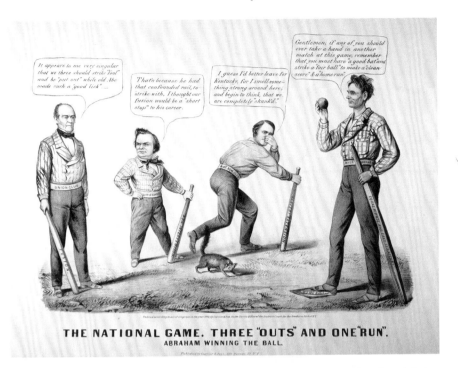

THE NATIONAL GAME. THREE "OUTS" AND ONE "RUN".
ABRAHAM WINNING THE BALL.

In this 1860 cartoon called *Winning the Ball*, Abraham Lincoln (*far right*) is shown with his opponents (*l to r*) John Bell, Stephen A. Douglas, and John C. Breckinridge. The question of states' rights and slavery in the territories, which Davis believed should be unconditional in favor of slave owners, finally came to a head with the presidential election of 1860. The Democratic Party separated into Northern and Southern factions, bringing victory to Lincoln and the Republican Party without the support of a single Southern state.

"I do not see why this eye has not burst," said Dr. Hayes, an eye specialist, as told in *Jefferson Davis: An American Patriot.* For weeks, Davis was forced to lie in a darkened room. Gradually, his health returned. After an extended family vacation in mid-year, he returned to his senatorial duties.

The leading voice among Southern Democrats, Davis battled a leader of the Northern Dems. Stephen A. Douglas opposed Davis's desire to grant slave owners absolute rights in the West. Davis also argued with Republicans over Kansas, which was on a path to becoming a free state. He was infuriated by an event in Harpers Ferry, Virginia, on October 16, 1859. That day, abolitionist John Brown led a raid of a federal armory, hoping to use the weapons to incite a massive slave rebellion. The U.S. military squelched Brown's attempt, but in the raid's aftermath, Davis took forceful action.

Early in 1860, the senator put forth the Davis Resolutions concerning the rights of slaveholders and the Southern states. Led by Davis, Southern Democrats urged Northern Democrats to help pass the resolutions, and they indeed were passed in May 1860. The rift between Northerners and Southerners, even within the Democratic Party, grew wider. In fact, the party split into two: the Northern Democrats and the State Rights Democrats. Each nominated its own candidates for president in 1860—Douglas for the former and John C. Breckinridge for the latter.

In November, neither candidate stood a chance against the increasingly popular Republican Party. A moderate on the slavery issue, Republican candidate Abraham Lincoln was not an abolitionist but did oppose the spread of slavery to new territories. Due largely to the antislavery sentiment that was sweeping the North—and because the Northern states were more populous than the Southern states—Lincoln won 180 electoral votes. Breckinridge dominated the Southern voting but finished second with only 72 electoral votes.

Southerners could not accept a Republican in the White House. Wrote Davis biographer William C. Davis: "Despite all protestations to the contrary, Lincoln's election was seen as the prelude to a direct attack on slavery and Southern rights. Politicians ranted, editors verbalized, ministers pontificated, and the ground swell of paranoia after this single event achieved what decades of Southern extremists had failed to accomplish. Secession, at least in the lower South, was inevitable."

President of the Confederate States

After the 1860 election, Lincoln insisted that he had no intention of ending slavery in the South. But at the polls, Northerners had shown their disdain for the Southern way of life. The antislavery Republican Party was now in power, and slaveholders felt threatened. The *Richmond Examiner* stated with alarm, "A party founded on the single sentiment…of hatred of African slavery, is now the controlling power."

Throughout the South, politicians and citizens railed for a break from the United States. On December 20, 1860, South Carolina became the first state to secede from the Union. On January 9, 1861, Davis's own state, Mississippi, seceded, too. In the following weeks, Florida, Alabama, Georgia, Louisiana, and Texas all followed suit—even before Lincoln had been sworn in as president.

With Mississippi no longer part of the Union, Davis needed to resign as U.S. senator. Yet, he was not anxious to leave Washington, preferring instead to assess the capital city's political situation. Davis supported secession, but unlike many of his angry constituents, he understood that the Southern states should not antagonize the Union. The former secretary of war knew that the South would be outmatched should the two sides ever wage war. The North had more people and, unlike the Southern states, its own army.

On January 21, 1861, after suffering from a migraine headache for a week, Davis finally delivered his senatorial farewell address. Dressed in black, Davis spoke to a packed audience in the Senate galleries. Wrote Davis biographer Allen Tate, "Under his high cheek-bones lay deep hollows; these and the square jaws and protruding chin gave the whole face a look of extreme emaciation—and of iron will."

In his speech, Davis discussed Mississippi's secession: "I do think she has justifiable cause, and I approve of her act." But he wanted to depart on the best of terms: "I hope, and they hope, for peaceable relations with you, though we must part." As he bid his final farewell, loud, heartfelt applause rained down for the respected statesman.

Still in great pain, Davis spent the next few days writing letters and telegrams to leaders of the Southern states. He implored them not to act or react violently toward the Union. In a letter to former president and friend Franklin Pierce, Davis said, "Civil War has only horror for me."

REBEL STATES CHOOSE THEIR LEADER

Soon, Davis and his family packed up their belongings and moved back to their Brierfield plantation. At age 52 and in poor health, Davis could have a few weeks of rest and relaxation. But he knew that hard times lay ahead. Each seceded state needed to form its own army, and Davis had already been selected as the major general of the Army of Mississippi. He had filled a similar role, with great success, during the Mexican-American War. Southern state leaders were also considering Davis for a more important position.

In a letter to Davis, South Carolina governor Francis Pickens stated that leaders of the Southern states were going to meet in Montgomery, Alabama. One of their top priorities, Pickens wrote, would be to elect "a Commander-in-Chief for the States and assess the States their quota in army and men and money. . . . Allow me to say that I think you are the proper man to be selected. . . ."

Others might have been flattered by the governor's assertion or inspired with visions of grandeur. Davis, though, did not want to shoulder such a heavy responsibility. Organizing Mississippi's militia, as he discovered while in Jackson, in late January, would be challenging enough. The troops were not even close to being prepared for war, should such a conflict develop.

In early February 1861, delegates from the seven seceded states met in Montgomery and drafted the Constitution of the Confederate States of America. Though similar to the U.S. Constitution, the Confederate version gave more power to individual states than to the central Confederate government. It also included specific protections for the institution of slavery (although it maintained the ban on international slave trading).

Delegates also discussed who should be the president and vice president of the Confederate States of America (the Confederacy). The two favorites for the presidency were Davis and Howell Cobb, a former governor of Georgia and a former Speaker of the House. Cobb made it clear that he did not want the job. Although Davis dreaded the position, too, he did not take himself out of the running like Cobb did. Robert Toombs, a vocal, driven man who had represented Georgia in the U.S. Senate, was another candidate. His addiction to alcohol, however, made him a less than ideal choice.

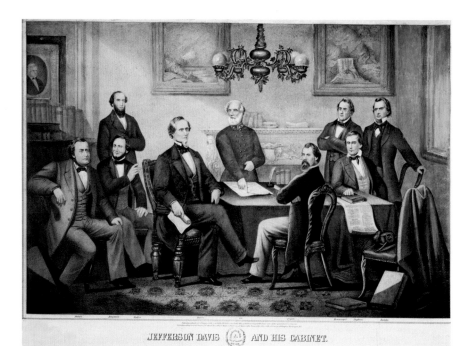

JEFFERSON DAVIS AND HIS CABINET

Davis was very popular, even receiving many votes at the presidential convention of 1860, although his friends had announced that he did not desire the nomination. Just days after resigning from the Senate following Mississippi's secession from the Union, Davis was named president of the Confederate States of America. Here, he is pictured with his cabinet, along with General Robert E. Lee, in the council chamber in Richmond.

The delegates liked Davis not only because of his qualifications but because he was universally respected. He was not an extremist who would alienate those within and outside the Confederacy. Whether Davis liked it or not, the delegates decided that he should lead the Confederate States of America. In a unanimous vote, they elected him provisional president. (In November 1861, the citizens of the Confederate states would cast their votes for president.) According to historian Samuel Eliot Morison, as recounted in *The Iron Will of Jefferson Davis,* the Mississippi statesman was the best man for the job. "In 1861 few on either side doubted that [Davis] was abler than Lincoln.

. . . Courage, patience and integrity were his; only perception and inner harmony were wanting to make him a great man."

In addition to Davis, the delegates elected Alexander H. Stephens of Georgia as vice president. A feisty, emotionally erratic man, Stephens would state in a speech in March 1861, "Our new government is founded . . . upon the great truth that the negro is not equal to the white man. . . ."

After receiving a telegram on February 10, which informed him that he had been elected president, Davis reluctantly accepted. Davis traveled to Montgomery. Along the way, he made more than two dozen speeches to Southerners who were elated by their new independence. After taking the oath of office on February 18, 1861, Davis got to work.

PRELUDE TO A WAR

Over the tumultuous course of his four-year presidency, Davis would antagonize colleagues with stubbornness and dictatorial leadership. But in the beginning, he made prudent decisions. To appease the seceded states, he chose a member of each state (except his own Mississippi) to comprise his six-member cabinet. They would be among his closest advisers. Davis also worked to bolster the Confederacy's military. He drew up war plans (just in case) on his own, and he organized the production of war materials, such as artillery, gunpowder, and naval vessels.

In the spring of 1861, both Davis and Lincoln tried to woo the eight slave states that had not yet seceded. These included Virginia, Arkansas, North Carolina, and Tennessee in the South as well as "border slave states" Missouri, Kentucky, Maryland, and Delaware. None of these states wanted to secede until after they saw what direction President Lincoln would lead the Union.

In Lincoln's inaugural address on March 4, 1861, he declared that he would not interfere with slavery in the 15 slave states, nor did he plan to invade the South. However, Lincoln considered secession to be an act of rebellion, and

DAVIS'S VICE PRESIDENT

Several weeks after being sworn into the office of vice president of the Confederate States of America, Alexander Hamilton Stephens delivered his controversial "Cornerstone" speech in Savannah, Georgia. "Our new government is founded," Stephens exclaimed, "its cornerstone rests, upon the great truth that the negro is not equal to the white man; that slavery—subordination to the superior race—is his natural and normal condition."

Jefferson Davis was upset that his new vice president shifted the focus of the rebellion from the issue of states' rights to that of slavery. The relationship between these two men only worsened during the course of the war.

Stephens had not originally supported secession and, in fact, voted against it. He felt that a compromise could still be reached in the U.S. Congress to save the Union and permit the continuation of slavery in the South. However, when his state of Georgia seceded, Stephens threw his support behind the Confederacy.

Throughout the war, Davis and Stephens were at odds over several of Davis's policies, including military decisions and the drafting of Confederate troops. Communication between the two finally broke down on March 16, 1864, when Stephens publicly expressed his opposition to Davis's actions in a speech to the Georgia legislature.

Stephens was arrested after the war and imprisoned for five months at Fort Warren, Massachusetts. With the defeat of the Confederacy and the emancipation of slaves, Stephens's cornerstone crumbled.

he urged the seceded states to rejoin the Union. Moreover, he declared that the Confederates must keep their hands off U.S. property, including military posts that happened to lie in the Confederate states.

After Lincoln's inauguration, Davis sent a commission to Washington. In a communication to the Department of State, they wrote: ". . . the Confederate government desires a 'peaceful solution' of all pending disputes [and] wishes to make no demand not founded in 'strict justice'. . . ." The Union wanted peace, too. However, miscommunication about a fort changed everything. In fact, the dispute over Fort Sumter in South Carolina ignited the Civil War.

DAVIS ATTACKS FORT SUMTER

The Confederates wanted the Union to evacuate Fort Sumter because the fort's soldiers guarded Charleston Harbor, which was a key port for the Confederate states. U.S. secretary of state William H. Seward, through indirect and unauthorized negotiations, indicated that the United States was willing to evacuate the fort. But President Lincoln thought otherwise. In fact, Lincoln informed South Carolina governor Francis Pickens that the United States was sending ships filled with nonmilitary supplies to Fort Sumter.

When Davis found out that these supply ships were headed to Fort Sumter, he realized that the Union had no intention of giving up the fort. He responded with a brazen and monumental decision. He sent a telegram to Brigadier General P.G.T. Beauregard, ordering him to issue a surrender notice to U.S. soldiers. Three of Beauregard's aides rowed to the fort in the wee hours of April 12 to deliver this message: If the Union did not surrender Fort Sumter, the Confederates would fire upon it. Major Robert Anderson refused to surrender.

At 4:30 A.M. on April 12, Confederate troops opened fire on Fort Sumter, and they continued the assault for 34 hours.

When the Union would not evacuate Fort Sumter, Jefferson Davis ordered the Confederates to open fire on the fort. With his ammunition on fire and supplies depleted, Union major Robert Anderson surrendered. Although this assault was not a deciding battle, it was seen as a declaration of war, launching one of the bloodiest wars in history.

Finally, Union troops raised a white flag—the sign of surrender. Despite the onslaught, no person was killed, just one pack animal. Davis, still dreading war despite his bold assault, tried to downplay the attack. He said to Varina, as she recounted in her memoir, "Separation is not yet of necessity final—there has been no blood spilled more precious than that of a mule."

But millions of people, in the North and South, did not see it that way. Blinded by hatred for the other side, they saw the attack as an act of war. President Lincoln used the event to convince young men to volunteer for armed service. On April 15, he issued a proclamation calling for 75,000 militia-

DAVIS AND LINCOLN

Future presidents Jefferson Davis and Abraham Lincoln were born in Kentucky cabins less than 100 miles apart. From that point, the lives of the two men would not intersect again until after four years of war.

Davis was sent to fine schools (including West Point) and served with distinction in the military during the Mexican-American War. He was a member of both houses of Congress, and he was appointed secretary of war by President Franklin Pierce. In contrast, Lincoln was self-educated, had very limited military experience, and served only one term in the House of Representatives.

Not only did the two men differ in life experience, but their appearance and personalities sharply contrasted. Davis had the bearing of a military man. He stood ramrod straight and gave the impression of being unapproachable. Lincoln, on the other hand, was lanky with poor posture. He was very approachable and enjoyed relaying jokes and funny stories to those around him.

Both men faced monumental challenges when they were given the reins of their countries. Davis had to create a government from scratch while raising an army to defend the Confederacy from Northern invasion. Lincoln had to take the many political and social factions in the North and mold them together to meet the greatest challenge in the history of the United States.

In his responsibility as commander in chief, Davis's West Point education and military experience actually were a hindrance to success. During the course of the conflict,

(continues)

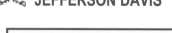

(continued)

Davis failed to name a competent general in charge of running the war. As a consequence, he spent as much time conducting the war as leading his country. In contrast, Lincoln searched for a strong military commander to assume the reins of the army. After many failures, he finally found the right man in Ulysses S. Grant.

Following the defeat of the Confederacy, the paths of both presidents once again crossed when Lincoln traveled to Richmond and sat at Davis's desk. Though these two leaders had shared many similar experiences during the war, this was as close as the two would come. Lincoln was assassinated only 11 days later in what Davis proclaimed as one of the darkest days for the South.

men. Soon, 200,000 men would be under arms in the United States.

The Confederates got stronger, too. The four remaining Southern slave states—Virginia, Arkansas, North Carolina, and Tennessee—joined the Confederacy between April 17 and June 8. Despite Davis's urgings, the border slave states—Missouri, Kentucky, Maryland, and Delaware—remained in the Union. However, many men in the latter four states would fight with the armies of the South. Davis discovered that huge numbers of Confederate men were willing to fight to preserve the Southern way of life. After he asked for 100,000 men to enlist for 12 months, some 300,000 volunteered.

On April 29, Davis spoke to the Confederacy's provisional congress. He continued to preach peace: "We feel that our cause is just and holy; we protest solemnly in the face of mankind that we desire peace at any sacrifice save that of honor and independence; we seek no conquest. . . ." He concluded, ". . . all we ask is to be let alone. . . ." As soon as Lincoln stopped trying to keep the seceded states in the Union, he said, the "sword will drop from our grasp."

But Lincoln would never stop trying, and thousands of Southerners would clutch their weapons until their final breath. The Civil War—the most devastating war in American history—loomed ahead.

Civil War Erupts

Often when a nation approaches war, patriotic excitement sweeps the land. Such was the case in the spring and summer of 1861. Two weeks after the attack on Fort Sumter, 100,000 Unionists staged a raucous rally in New York City. Down south, musicians cheerily played the new anthem of the South, "Dixie." Southern volunteers said good-bye to their loved ones as they set off for military training. Along the way, "Southern belles" cheered them on. As noted in *The Civil War Chronicle,* a journalist traveling in the South saw "crowds of armed men singing and promenading the streets, the battle blood running through their veins—that hot oxygen which is called 'the flush of victory' on the cheek."

Davis had neither the time nor the inclination to share their enthusiasm. Wrote historian Robert Paul Jordan in *The*

Civil War: "Davis, age 52, now stood at the Confederacy's head, trying to run a revolution by constitutional means, trying to build a victorious central government for 11 sovereign states. So sensitive that even a child's disapproval could upset him, so high-minded that compromise came hard to him, he gave himself completely to his country, hiding a flaming courage behind a stiff and chilly dignity."

Davis just wanted the Confederacy to be left alone, but "war fever" was infecting both nations. In the North, abolitionists called for war against the South and the end to slavery. Many Northern papers urged President Lincoln to restore the Union—by force. On April 19, 1861, as a Massachusetts regiment moved through Baltimore, Maryland, to guard Washington, D.C., it was attacked by Southern loyalists. Thirteen people died.

Though war had yet to begin on land, skirmishes raged in the waters. On April 19, Lincoln ordered a blockade of all Confederate ports. This would cut off the Confederacy from the outside world and crimp its economy. In response, Davis called for Southern ship owners to attack Northern merchant ships and confiscate their cargo. To Lincoln, this was nothing short of piracy.

LAYING PLANS FOR WAR

As hostilities heated up, both sides made plans for war. Because the industrialized Union was so rich in resources, Davis had no intention of invading the North. Instead, he believed in fighting a defensive war. He hoped that the North would grow weary of fighting the tenacious Southern soldiers and eventually give up the fight, letting the Confederates live in peace. Davis also hoped that European powers would side with the South because of their need for cotton. Many Southerners had faith that Great Britain and France would supply arms and munitions to the Confederacy in exchange for cotton. This wouldn't be the case.

Beginning on April 19, 1861, Abraham Lincoln ordered a blockade of all Confederate ports. His strategy required the closure of 3,500 miles of Confederate coastline and 12 major ports, including the port of New Orleans, Louisiana (*above*). Here, paddle streamers sit in docks where Confederate troops placed a chain across the river to prevent Union troops from capturing the city by sea. The chain was cut and the city was captured by the Union.

Davis created military units in strategic locations throughout the South, and he sent troops to each. The Confederates correctly assumed that if the North attacked, it would do so in Virginia, which was just south of the nation's capital. Thinking they should be close to the front lines, Davis and the Confederate leadership decided to move their capital to Richmond, Virginia. Davis arrived in Richmond on May 29, and his wife and children (Maggie, Jeff, and Joseph) reached their new home a few days later.

Virginia governor John Letcher appointed 54-year-old Robert E. Lee—an old friend of Davis's—to command volunteers in his state. After more than 30 years with the U.S. Army, Lee was now loyal to the state his father had once governed. Lee would become the most celebrated Confederate general of the Civil War.

By late May, Davis had stationed more than 20,000 troops along a creek named Bull Run near Manassas, Virginia. Brigadier General P.G.T. Beauregard, who had led the assault at Fort Sumter, commanded this massive force. Up through mid-July, Northerners urged the U.S. Army to storm into Virginia and put a swift end to the rebellion. Lincoln, too, became anxious. Back in April, many volunteers had signed up for 90-day enlistments, which were about to expire. General Irvin McDowell felt his amateur soldiers were not ready for battle. But Lincoln ordered McDowell to attack, and the general led his 30,000 troops from Washington to Bull Run.

THE BLOODY REALITY

Those troops who considered this an exciting adventure were gravely naïve. On July 21, at Bull Run, the Northerners clashed ferociously with Beauregard's 22,000 men and Confederate general Joseph E. Johnston's 12,000 troops. "The air is full of fearful noises," wrote a witness, as recounted in *The Civil War Chronicle.* "There is smoke, dust, wild talking, shouting, hissings, howlings, explosions."

Davis himself journeyed to the battlefield. Like everyone else, he was shocked by the number of casualties. Some 2,900 Union soldiers were killed, and nearly 2,000 Confederates lost their lives. The undertrained, overmatched Union forces retreated back to Washington. Davis wished his soldiers could have followed them and overrun Washington, which might have ended the war. But the Confederate troops were disorganized and could not pursue the enemy.

Southerners celebrated their triumph at the Battle of Bull Run, but Davis worried about the larger war. The citizens of western Virginia did not support the Confederacy, and that area became a battleground. The Northerners won several battles in western Virginia before 1861 was over. (West Virginia would join the Union on June 20, 1863.)

The Confederates did win small battles in Virginia and Missouri in 1861. Their navy also made progress, constructing ironclad gunboats that could wreak havoc on the Union's

THE CONFEDERATE SOLDIER

Most young men who volunteered to fight in the Confederate armies did not do so to keep slavery as an institution in the South. Nor did they fight for a state's right to choose its own destiny. These were the ideals of the politicians, wealthy merchants, and plantation owners. The common soldier would never consider them important enough to die for. Young Southerners enlisted for many other reasons. Most importantly, they wanted to protect their families and possessions from the foreign invaders from the North.

They came to war dressed like professional soldiers, with new uniforms and accoutrements. At the start of the war, they carried as much as 100 pounds of baggage. It did not take long for them to realize the folly in all of these trappings. Due to long marches and short bursts of battle, they were better met carrying the least amount of clothes

wooden ships. However, the much larger U.S. Navy strengthened its naval blockade, further crimping the South's ability to trade with Europe. Davis also worried about the Mississippi River. The Confederate states of Arkansas and Texas and part of Louisiana were west of the Mississippi. Should the Union take control of the mighty river, the Confederacy would be split into two.

In the early months of 1862, the North focused its attention on the western Confederacy, just east of the Mississippi River. In February, Union general Ulysses S. Grant scored victories at Fort Henry and Fort Donelson in Tennessee. That

and equipment. Thus, the soldiers scattered their excess baggage along the route of march and kept the bare essentials: clothing on their back, a musket, a cartridge box, a canteen, and a blanket. They also carried a haversack to store a pipe, tobacco, and any food they were issued or could forage from the farms they passed.

During the latter stages of the war, resources dwindled throughout the South. For Confederate fighters, the only sources of food, clothing, shoes, and equipment came either from home or from the bodies of dead Union soldiers. Wrote G. H. Baskett in the *Confederate Veteran*, "Half clad, half armed, often half fed, without money and without price, the Confederate soldier fought against the resources of the world. When at last his flag was furled and his arms were grounded in defeat, the cause for which he had struggled was lost, but he had won the faceless victory of soldiership."

month, his troops occupied nearby Nashville, making it the first state capital to fall to Union troops.

On April 6, Confederate forces launched a surprise attack at the Battle of Shiloh in western Tennessee. Confederate commander General Albert Sidney Johnston was killed that day, but the Southern troops threw General Grant's men into disarray. "Whip 'em tomorrow, though," Grant said, as told in *The American Civil War*, and they did. Reinforced by the Army of Ohio, the Union troops counterattacked and forced the Confederates into retreat. The rain that fell on the Battle of Shiloh mixed with the spilled blood of the dead and injured. The number of casualties was horrific, with each side counting more than 1,700 dead and 8,000 wounded.

For Davis, April turned out to be devastating. On the 25th, Union warships captured strategically important New Orleans, Louisiana. The largest city in the Confederacy, it also included its most vital port. This is where the Mississippi River flowed into the Gulf of Mexico. After New Orleans fell, the South controlled only one fortified city on the river: Vicksburg, Mississippi. If that fell, the river—and likely the Confederate states west of it—would belong to the Union.

LEE'S EPIC BATTLES

Despite the disastrous news in the Western Theater, the most important events of 1862 took place in the East. The Union's main goal was to overrun Richmond and put an end to the war. To save the Confederacy, Davis insisted upon conscription. In April 1862, the Confederate Congress passed a law that forced able-bodied men age 18 to 35 to sign up for three years of military service. Many in the South protested Davis's decision and would begrudge him for the rest of the war.

In the spring of 1862, the Union's major general George B. McClellan amassed a huge army within several miles of Richmond. General Joseph E. Johnston commanded the Southern troops near the Confederate capital, but when he

One of the most decisive events in the war began on April 18 and continued until April 25. It resulted in the Union's capture of Confederate forts Jackson, St. Phillip, Livingston, Pike, and the city of New Orleans, as well as the destruction of all the enemy gunboats, rams, floating batteries, fire rafts, and other military equipment. Commander David Farragut was promoted to the rank of rear admiral, a rank not used in the U.S. Navy at that time.

was wounded, Davis made an important and wise decision. "General Lee," he told his close confidant, as told in *The Iron Will of Jefferson Davis,* "I am assigning to you the command of the Army."

A brilliant strategist, Lee believed that the best defense would be a good offense. Lee's Army of Northern Virginia attacked Union forces at Beaver Dam Creek, Gaines' Mill, and other locations, forcing McClellan's troops to retreat. During the Seven Days' Battles, the South suffered twice as many dead (3,500) and wounded (15,700) than the North. However, Lee saved Richmond—and the Confederacy.

Determined to capture Richmond, President Lincoln entrusted General John Pope with the task. On August 28–30, Pope's army met Lee's in the Second Battle of Bull Run. Casualties were heavy on both sides—more than 18,000 dead and wounded altogether—but the Union troops suffered more. The Confederates won the battle, forcing the enemy to retreat toward Washington.

Davis, suffering from migraines and looking frail, in 1862, was now excited about his army's successes. Immediately after Bull Run, Lee informed Davis that they should advance into Union territory for the first time. He believed that a victory in the North would demoralize U.S. citizens and convince European nations to recognize the Confederacy as its own nation. Indeed, Great Britain was considering intervening on the side of the South—although at the time, Davis did not know its intention.

Lee wanted to wage battle in Pennsylvania, but on September 17, McClellan's troops attacked Lee's men near Antietam Creek in Sharpsburg, Maryland. The Confederate soldiers lacked uniforms and proper weapons, but they had a fighting spirit. Wrote one eyewitness, as recounted in *How the North Won,* "They were the dirtiest men I ever saw, a most ragged, lean, and hungry set of wolves."

The battle lasted just one day, but it was the bloodiest day of fighting in American history—before or since. More than 3,600 men were killed, and more than 17,000 were wounded. The North suffered more casualties, but because Lee's men retreated all the way back to Confederate territory, the Union claimed a great moral victory.

FIGHTING MAD

Davis and his people were determined to continue the fight—especially after President Lincoln's Emancipation Proclamation, which he announced on September 22, 1862. Lincoln declared "that all persons held as slaves" within the rebellious states "are, and henceforward shall be free." The proclamation infuriated white Southerners, including Davis. They accused Lincoln of trying to instigate a slave rebellion in states that he could not occupy with troops. Some Southern lawmakers were

WHITE HOUSE OF THE CONFEDERACY

Neither Jefferson Davis nor the Confederacy owned the Confederate White House. Instead, the government rented it from the city of Richmond. Moreover, the White House was not even white but, instead, a gray stucco structure. In fact, it was sometimes called the Gray House. Back in 1818, Robert Mills designed the mansion for a wealthy banker named John Brockenbrough.

Davis and his family moved into the house in August 1861. As the war progressed, Davis began to conduct much of his business in his White House office. Politicians and military advisers frequented the mansion day and night as the war dragged on. Even in the midst of this daily bustle, Davis and his wife, Varina, attempted to provide a loving, warm family life.

Two of their children, William and Varina Anne, were born while living in the mansion. Tragedy struck, however, on April 30, 1864, when the couple's four-year-old son, Joseph, died after falling off a second-floor balcony.

Soon after the Davises fled from the mansion in April 1865, relic hunters descended on the house, leaving little behind. After the war, it was occupied by Union troops for several years before being turned into a school. It escaped a wrecking ball and, in 1896, became the home of the Museum of the Confederacy.

so incensed that they proposed the death sentence for any person who spoke against slavery.

Lincoln's proclamation certainly motivated the Confederate soldiers, who triumphed at the Battle of Fredericksburg in Virginia in December 1862. The Southern soldiers were so determined that Lee, as recounted in *The Iron Will of Jefferson Davis,* saw soldiers "weep with disappointment when commanded to retire in the face of withering fire."

Davis's armies were winning battles but at a terrible price. Since much of the fighting was in Virginia (or to the north in Maryland), Richmond teemed with recovering wounded soldiers. Young belles worked in hospital wards all day and then danced with lightly wounded soldiers at morale-boosting dances at night. The economic situation was so bad that Confederate currency was worthless. Such food staples as flour and vegetables were in short supply. In fact, Varina Davis was criticized for "hoarding" flour. More alarmingly, the South lacked metal for ammunition and medical supplies to treat the many wounded. Diseases such as scurvy and dysentery became epidemic.

On December 26, 1862, Davis addressed the Mississippi legislature in a motivational speech. He vilified the North as a "den of thieves." He defended the Confederacy's controversial conscription laws, which exempted large plantation owners from the draft: "It is the poor who save nations and make revolutions." He portrayed the South as an underdog holding its own against a great power: "the wonder is not that we have done little, but that we have done so much." And he expressed optimism for what lay ahead: "in all respects, moral as well as physical, we are better prepared than we were a year ago."

Southerners would have liked to believe their president, but the majority had their doubts.

Demise of the Confederacy

During the first three months of 1863, the North and South traded minor victories—all in Confederate territory. However, several nonmilitary events revealed the enormous toll the war was taking on the South. On March 13, an explosion occurred at an ammunition factory in Richmond. Some 50 workers were killed, most of whom were girls. The Confederacy was so starved for revenue that in April it established a variety of income and property taxes. This put an even greater burden on a populace that was sacrificing, struggling, and starving.

Southerners were so hungry that "bread riots" erupted in multiple Southern cities. On April 2, 1863, in Davis's city of Richmond, some 3,000 women marched down Main Street. Armed with guns and clubs, they demanded bread for their children. The women were so angry and desperate that they

Due to the Union blockades and plundering soldiers, thousands of people were going hungry. Desperation grew until, on April 2, 1863, a bread riot erupted. The rioters eventually dispersed after Davis threatened to have the militia fire on them. The riot ended peacefully, although 44 women and 29 men were arrested.

stormed stores and stole flour, meat, and other items. Davis himself implored the women to stop, but they ignored their president. They dispersed only after he threatened to have militiamen open fire on them.

The Union blockade and ravages of war were taking their toll on the South. Soldiers lacked guns, ammunition, and proper clothing. Railroad transportation was ineffective. Many farmers went off to war, leaving their farms unattended. Moreover, the Confederate army snatched animals from family farms to feed the soldiers, leaving the civilians without milk, eggs, and meat. The soldiers often took the farms' horses, too.

In the heart of winter, Davis spent three weeks touring the western front, where the news was bleak. It wouldn't be long, it appeared, until the Union took complete control of the Mississippi River. Confederate states west of the river would be isolated and lost to the Union. Davis learned that his beloved plantation in Mississippi, Brierfield, had been seized by Northern soldiers.

BLAMING DAVIS

Davis knew that the South could not win a long war. It was already barely surviving, and the Union seemed to have endless supplies of men and munitions. Davis's only hope was that his troops would score big wins in the East. With such successes, U.S. citizens might grow tired of the war and push for a peace settlement.

Fairly or not, many Southerners blamed Davis for the Confederacy's failings. Some accused him of being dictatorial and not listening to his congressmen and cabinet members. Others said he had neglected the war in the west, though in reality, he had too few soldiers to cover the South's vast territory. Some blamed Davis for appointing the wrong men to commander positions. Others cried that Davis should have done more to secure European nations as allies. In short, the South had taken on a war that it realistically could not win. But citizens needed to blame someone, and Davis was it.

Disillusioned by the war, more and more soldiers deserted from the Confederate armies. Yet most of the Southern troops maintained a fighting spirit, and in early May, they scored a stunning victory in Virginia. It had appeared that the Union would trounce the Confederates in the Battle of Chancellorsville. They not only boasted twice as many troops as the enemy (134,000 to 61,000), but the soldiers were better supplied. Nevertheless, General Lee's unconventional and aggressive actions confounded the Union troops. The North suffered 17,200 casualties and retreated from battle. The downside for the Confederates is that they had endured

SLAVES AS CONFEDERATE SOLDIERS?

From the beginning of the war, many Confederate officers chose slaves to act as their servants and personal attendants. They accompanied their masters on military campaigns and took care of their needs while in camp. Initially, slaves were not used in combat. As the war progressed, however, and the rebel armies were outnumbered by tens of thousands, Confederate congressmen frequently discussed the notion of impressing blacks into combat.

Many Southerners felt that it would be risky to place guns in the hands of slaves. Some thought that to reduce this threat, the slaves should be freed before joining the Confederate armies. Freeing large numbers of blacks, however, would cut down on the number of slaves remaining to work the fields. Further complicating matters, those freed blacks would most likely demand the freedom of their families as well.

Jefferson Davis was convinced that arming blacks was the only way to inject hope into the Confederates' failing cause. The measure went to the Confederate Congress in early 1865, and it passed both houses by March 8. It was too late, however, since General Robert E. Lee surrendered his army at Appomattox Court House a month later.

12,700 casualties, severely depleting their pool of troops. Moreover, Thomas "Stonewall" Jackson—the most revered Confederate general next to Lee—died on the battlefield.

THE GETTYSBURG CALAMITY

Lee advised Davis that they should follow up their victory with an attack in Union territory. He reasoned that another big, devastating loss for the North would force Lincoln to think about a peace settlement. Davis was reluctant to approve the plan, feeling that Confederate troops had absorbed enough recent punishment. But he finally agreed, and on July 1–3, the enemy engaged Lee's men on Northern soil in the bloodiest battle of the Civil War.

In Gettysburg, Pennsylvania, Lee's 71,000 troops took on General George Meade's 94,000 soldiers. Both sides suffered enormous casualties on the first two days of the battle. July 3 turned out disastrously for the Confederates. At one point, more than 12,000 Confederate soldiers charged against the center of the Union line on Cemetery Ridge. Through rifle and artillery fire, Union troops massacred large numbers of the helpless soldiers. By the end of the battle, 46,000 men had been killed, wounded, captured, or reported missing. More than 4,700 rebel soldiers died.

It turned out that Davis should have followed his own instincts and not listened to Lee's advice. Wrote historian Hamilton J. Eckenrode, "Davis has been blamed for preferring his own judgment to that of his generals, but in this case when he went against his judgment he made the mistake that decided the outcome of the war." Lee, blaming himself, offered to resign, but Davis was not willing to lose his best general.

The South suffered politically as well as militarily. While European nations had considered recognizing the Confederacy after its win at Chancellorsville, they backed off after Gettysburg. Wrote journalist Henry Adams to his father, "It is now conceded that all idea of intervention is at an end." Even Confederate vice president Alexander Stephens had given up on the war. Davis sent Stephens to Washington to discuss prisoner exchanges, but Stephens instead hoped to discuss peace with top officials. He never made it to the nation's capital.

DESPERATE TIMES

Davis was distraught over the Gettysburg conflict, and the news out West was not any better. Vicksburg, Mississippi, a major trading center on the Mississippi River, had been under siege for weeks. Union troops under the command of General Ulysses S. Grant trapped tens of thousands of Confederate soldiers and residents. Civilians lived in caves to avoid being shot, and they ate roasted rats to fend off starvation. Finally, on July 4, Confederate commander John C. Pemberton and his officers surrendered nearly 30,000 soldiers and about 60,000 muskets. The Union now controlled the Mississippi, meaning Davis could not help the Confederate territories west of the river.

Throughout the South, people urged their president to surrender. But Davis refused to give up, thinking that the worst of the fighting was over and that the South could bounce back. Smartly, he decided to ship huge amounts of cotton to the West Indies, where it was traded for arms and supplies.

Despite 18,000 casualties, the Confederates prevailed in the Battle of Chickamauga in Georgia in September 1863. Forty thousand Union soldiers retreated to Chattanooga, Tennessee, and Confederate general Braxton Bragg's troops besieged the city. Spirits soared throughout the South. However, the elation turned out to be temporary, as Union reinforcements broke the siege. The Battle of Chattanooga in November 1863, further deflated Southern spirits. By defeating Bragg's Army of Tennessee, the U.S. Army created a clear pathway to the Deep South.

By late 1863, the Confederacy lay on its deathbed. The young nation faced bankruptcy, and its people were poor and starving. Pathetically understaffed and under-supplied, hospitals could offer little help to thousands of wounded and ill soldiers. The situation could not have been bleaker. But Davis, despite suffering his own physical pain and exhaustion, would not give up the fight.

DAVIS: MORE SACRIFICE NEEDED

In an address to the Confederate Congress on December 7, 1863, Davis expressed the numerous woes facing the South. But he also claimed that the "enemy has been checked" and the Confederate army was "in all respects in better condition than at any previous period of the war." Davis called for even greater sacrifices. All able-bodied men should enroll in the army, he said. Older men could handle noncombat roles, such as guard duty and searching for deserters. Slaves, he proposed, could serve as cooks and laborers.

Congress responded. No longer could wealthy men hire substitutes to serve for them; every man would have to contribute to the war effort. Even the crippled would work, as Congress established an Invalid Corps. Men no longer fit for duty would take on desk jobs and other "easy" tasks.

In the later months of 1863, Davis seemed to turn to religion for comfort. "He went often to church," wrote Davis biographers Herman Hattaway and Richard E. Beringer. "The tender, typically hidden, side of his nature was more manifest. He pardoned criminals and commuted death sentences…. Davis exuded mercy even as he himself ever more needed it."

As Christmas approached, Southerners scrounged to find food for their holiday meal. "'The Ham the Lamb the Jelly & the Jam' are now of the past," Davis's friend told him, as recounted in *Jefferson Davis, Confederate President*. "It is now 'Small Hominy sometimes called Grits.'"

"HELL ON EARTH"

Little fighting took place during the winters of the Civil War. But everyone knew that the Union Army's surges would begin again in the spring of 1864. Not only was the Confederacy broke, it lacked manpower. By the thousands, Southern men had been killed, disabled, or stricken with debilitating diseases. Large numbers of soldiers deserted and returned to their families, and the Confederacy did not have the means to stop them.

Tens of thousands of soldiers, on both sides, were also held as prisoners of war. Prisoner exchanges occurred throughout much of the war, although General Grant was against the practice. He felt that released Confederate prisoners would become soldiers again and would thus extend the war. Prisoner exchanges came to a halt in the spring of 1864—and with tragic results. The trouble started on April 12, 1864, when Confederate troops under Major General Nathan Bedford Forrest massacred black Union soldiers at Fort Pillow, Tennessee. President Lincoln responded by demanding from the Confederacy that black POWs be treated as humanely as white POWs. Davis refused, and as a result, the Union ended prisoner exchanges.

That decision presented two problems for Davis. One, his much-needed soldiers were sitting idle in Union prisons; and two, the Confederacy did not have the means to care for the tens of thousands of Union prisoners. Andersonville, in western Georgia, was the most notorious Confederate prison camp.

Meant to hold 13,000 men when it first opened in early 1864, Andersonville's population swelled to 33,000 during the sweltering month of August. Conditions were barbaric. Prisoners were exposed to the elements and drank polluted war. They suffered from hunger and malnutrition, and diseases swept through the camp. In his diary, Sergeant David Kennedy of the Ohio Cavalry described it as "hell on earth where it takes 7 of its occupants to make a shadow."

Nearly 13,000 prisoners would die at Andersonville, and many more would succumb at other Confederate POW camps.

The Andersonville prison camp in Georgia was the largest of the military prisons used during the Civil War. Captured Union soldiers were brought here from February 1864 until May 1865. The Confederacy was unable to provide adequate care for the captives, thus the prisoners of war were kept in debilitating conditions. About 13,000 men would die from disease, poor sanitation, malnutrition, or exposure to the elements.

When Northerners learned how horribly the South was treating their soldiers, they vowed vengeance.

THE DEATH OF LITTLE JOSEPH

On April 30, the Davis family suffered its own horror. Four-year-old Joseph, the second youngest of the Davises' four children, fell off the second-floor balcony of the Confederate White House. He landed on the ground's brick surface, and he died a few minutes later. Each night, Joseph had knelt next to his father and said his prayers. Now he was gone. It was the second time in 10 years that Jefferson and Varina had lost a young son. Well into the night, Varina—who was about seven months pregnant—screamed in grief. But Davis showed little outward emotion. As told in *Jefferson Davis: The Man and His Hour,* he muttered over and over, "Not mine, oh, Lord, but thine."

The next afternoon, Davis received a letter from General Lee. The enemy was planning an attack, Lee wrote, and he needed Davis to provide him with reinforcements. Davis stared blankly at the paper before him. He could not think clearly. "I must have this day with my little child," he uttered, as recounted in *Jefferson Davis: The Man and His Hour.* He then went upstairs and spent the rest of the day and night in his room. As he did when his son Samuel had died, he paced the floor throughout the night.

ONE LAST GLIMMER OF HOPE

When he returned to work the next day, Davis faced the Confederacy's gravest situation yet. General Lee was correct: General Grant was preparing a massive assault on Lee's troops in Virginia, with the goal of capturing Richmond. That was only one-third of the problem. In northwest Virginia, in the Shenandoah Valley, Union general Phil Sheridan was planning his own push toward Richmond. And in Chattanooga, Tennessee, General William T. Sherman was concocting his march through Georgia. It was all part of Grant's three-pronged plan to overwhelm the Confederacy, capture Richmond, and end the war on the Union's terms.

It did not seem like the South stood a chance, but again, Lee's brilliance and the rebels' spirit shone through. In northern Virginia, Grant led the Army of the Potomac (118,000 strong) into an area called the Wilderness. Lee's Army of Northern Virginia boasted only 60,000 troops, but on May 5, they engaged the enemy. Over the next few weeks, the two sides fought ferociously on several Virginia battlefields. At the Battle of Cold Harbor on June 3, 1864, the Union lost 7,000 men in just a few hours, making it the worst slaughter of the war.

On multiple occasions, President Davis rode his horse to the battlefields. "[H]e was an inspiration to every soul who saw him," wrote one of his generals, as told in *Jefferson Davis: Confederate President*. "He did not once interfere, suggest or order anything, but he was there demonstrating his readiness. . . ." When the Wilderness campaign concluded, the Confederacy had lost 20,000 men to the Union's 60,000.

Davis was also encouraged by events in the West, where Sherman struggled to lead his 100,000 troops across mountainous terrain. In the Battle of Kennesaw Mountain on June 27, Confederate general Joseph E. Johnston's army inflicted 3,000 casualties while absorbing 1,000.

Once again, Davis held out hope for success. With the Union losing men and gaining little progress, Northerners were becoming frustrated. He felt that if his troops could fend off Union advancements until November, U.S. citizens would vote Lincoln out of office. They likely would vote for a candidate of the Democratic Party, whose platform called for the immediate end of the war and a negotiated settlement with the Confederacy. Had such events played out, Davis might have been hailed as a hero and a savior of the South.

THE UNION BUSTS THROUGH

The Confederates, however, simply did not have the strength to last that long. By July, Sherman's army was moving steadily toward Atlanta. Davis lost patience with the conservative tactics of General Johnston. He replaced him with John Bell Hood—a young, aggressive, almost reckless general. General Lee told Davis not to make the switch, but the president did not listen. On July 20, with the Union just three miles from Atlanta, Hood attacked at Peachtree Creek. But the Northerners held, and the Confederates fell back. After a series of battles, the Union occupied Atlanta on September 2—and burned down the city.

Showing his support, Davis visited Georgia in September. On the 23rd, he addressed citizens in a speech in Macon: "The son of a Georgian, who fought through the first Revolution, I would be untrue to myself if I should forget the State in her day of peril. . . ." Davis remained optimistic, declaring: "What, though misfortune has befallen our arms from Decatur to Jonesboro, our cause is not lost. Sherman cannot keep up his long line of communication, and retreat sooner or later, he must."

But Sherman would not retreat. In fact, the Confederates would march through Georgia unimpeded. Meanwhile, General Sheridan was breaking through in Shenandoah Valley in western Virginia. After defeating Jubal Early's forces in a major battle on October 19, the Union army took control of the valley.

With their nation crumbling around them, Southerners clamored for Lee to replace Davis as leader of the Confederacy. Lee was not interested, and he stood by his old friend. When asked about Davis's competency as president, Lee said he knew of no man who could have done better.

Desperate for manpower, Davis in November 1864 asked Congress to purchase 40,000 slaves for the military. He would not arm the slaves but instead use them in noncombatant roles. "Until our white population shall prove insufficient for the armies," he told Congress, "to employ as a soldier the negro . . . would scarcely be deemed wise or advantageous. . . ." However, he added: "But should the alternative ever be presented of subjugation, or of the employment of the slave as a soldier, there seems no reason to doubt what should then be our decision."

In other words, Davis would employ slaves as soldiers if the Confederacy reached a point where it had no other choice. (That day would come in early 1865.) He also said that slaves who joined the military, even in noncombatant roles, should be granted their freedom after they were discharged. Events had become so desperate in the South that Davis—the great protector of slavery—was granting slaves their freedom.

"A BARREN WASTE"

By the end of 1864, Union armies were laying the South to waste. Generals Grant and Sherman believed that to decisively end the Civil War, they needed to break the South militarily, economically, and psychologically. From Atlanta, Sherman's troops began their infamous March to the Sea. From November 15 to December 22, they stormed toward Savannah, Georgia, burning infrastructure and crops and killing livestock.

Prior to Sherman's march, General Sheridan began his devastation of the Shenandoah Valley, eliminating the primary food supply for Lee's army. Sheridan followed the orders of Grant, who, according to the biography *Grant*, had stated, "Do all the damage to railroads and crops you can. Carry off stock of all descriptions and negroes so as to prevent further planting. If the War is to last another year we want the Shenandoah valley to remain a barren waste."

By the end of 1864, the Confederate economy was so ravaged that, in Richmond, flour sold for $1,500 a barrel. As told in *Generals in Blue and Gray,* one woman stated, "You can carry your money in a market basket and bring home your provisions in your purse."

After a year of intense national and personal suffering, Varina Davis was determined to celebrate Christmas at the Confederate White House. In the *New York World* years later, Varina wrote of the 1864 holiday: "On Christmas morning the children awoke early and came in to see their toys. They were followed by the negro women, who one after another 'caught' us by wishing us a merry Christmas before we could say it to them, which gave them a right to a gift. Of course, there was a present for every one, small though it might be. . . ."

It would be the Davis's last Christmas at the White House. In fact, war would soon separate Jefferson from the rest of his family.

FIGHT TO THE FINISH

Early in 1865, both Davis and Lincoln were ready to discuss a peaceful end to this horrific war. On February 3, Lincoln and Secretary of State William Seward met on the steamboat *River Queen* with three Confederate commissioners, led by Vice President Alexander Stephens. According to the book *Conversations with Lincoln,* during negotiations in the boat's saloon, Stephens asked, "[I]s there no way of putting an end to the present trouble, and bringing about a restoration of the general

SHERMAN'S MARCH

After he captured Atlanta, Union general William T. Sherman decided to march his army to the sea. From November 15 to December 21, 1864, his army cut a 60-mile-wide swath through the heart of Georgia, exacting an estimated $100 million in damage. What his troops did not consume, they destroyed. His intent from the beginning of the march was to make "Georgia howl."

Two Southern diarists wrote about the effect of this march on the civilian population. Mary Chestnut noted, "They say no living thing is found in Sherman's track, only chimneys, like telegraph poles, to carry the news of Sherman's army backward." Eliza Andrews wrote in her diary:

> About three miles from Sparta we struck the "Burnt Country," as it is well named by the natives, and then I could better

good feeling and harmony . . . ?" Lincoln replied, "there is but one way I know of and that is for those who are resisting the laws of the Union to cease that resistance."

Lincoln emphatically stated that he would end the war only if the Union was restored. The Confederate president would not accept these terms. Davis would (later in the month) grant freedom to the slaves who would serve in the armed forces, but he would *not* accept the dissolution of the Confederate States of America. The South, he decided, would fight to the finish.

The end was near. By March, General Grant's army had nearly encircled the Confederate capital of Richmond. Davis stayed, but he sent Varina and their children to Charlotte, North Carolina. On April 2, Davis heard from General Lee.

understand the wrath and desperation of these poor people. I almost felt as if I should like to hang a Yankee myself. There was hardly a fence left standing all the way from Sparta to Gordon. The fields were trampled down and the road was lined with carcasses of horses, hogs, and cattle that the invaders, unable either to consume or to carry away with them, had wantonly shot down to starve out the people and prevent them from making their crops. The stench in some places was unbearable.... The dwellings that were standing all showed signs of pillage, and on every plantation we saw the charred remains of the gin-house and packing-screw, while here and there, lone chimney-stacks, "Sherman's Sentinels," told of homes laid in ashes.

Sherman offered no apology for the suffering caused by his army during his March to the Sea. In a postwar speech he stated, "War is hell."

Union troops, Lee's message read, had broken through the Confederate defense and were headed to Richmond. Instead of giving up, Davis decided to relocate his nation's capital. He told his cabinet members to pack up government records; they were headed south to Danville, Virginia. The "Richmond and Danville" happened to be the only railroad line still in operation.

The citizens of Richmond frantically evacuated the city. To hinder the enemy, Confederate soldiers set fire to bridges, the armory, and the warehouses that stored supplies. These fires spread out of control, and much of the city went up in flames.

After arriving safely in Danville, Davis set up his offices and awaited further word from Lee. This time, the general reported even worse news: His army had suffered heavy casualties and was now surrounded by Grant's troops. Lee had performed miracles on the battlefield before, and Davis hoped he could somehow escape the Union general's grasp. But on April 9, a messenger informed the Confederate president that Lee had surrendered.

That morning, in a final showdown at Appomattox Court House, Lee's forces had been badly outnumbered. Realizing that the situation was hopeless, Lee submitted to defeat. As told in *Battlefields of the Civil War,* Lee said "there is nothing left for me to do but to go and see General Grant, and I would rather die a thousand deaths." Upon the despondent general's surrender, Grant mercifully promised him a large supply of food to feed his starving troops.

Upon reading about Lee's surrender, bystanders watched Davis "silently weep bitter tears." Recalled eyewitness Bob Lee, as noted in *The Long Surrender,* "He seemed quite broken at the moment by this tangible evidence of the loss of his army and the misfortunes of its General. All of us, respecting his great grief, withdrew…."

ON THE RUN

Soon, scouts informed Davis and his cabinet that Union forces were closing in on Danville. Davis could have stayed and surrendered, headed to Charlotte to be with his family, or simply run for his life. But instead, he instructed his remaining Confederate leaders to go with him to Greensboro, North Carolina. That's where the rest of the Confederate army, under General Johnston, was stationed. Incredibly, Davis still was not ready to admit defeat!

In Greensboro, Generals Johnston, Beauregard, and Breckinridge all agreed that further resistance would be pointless. Once Davis arrived, Johnston and Beauregard tried to convince their president that the war should end. As described in *The Longest Night,* Johnston told Davis that "our people are tired of the war, feel themselves whipped, and will not fight. Our country is overrun, its military resources greatly diminished, while the enemy's military power and resources were never greater and may be increased to any extent desired.... My small force is melting away like snow before the sun."

Certainly, Davis should have surrendered at this point. Instead, he, his cabinet members, and a thousand soldiers headed to Charlotte, North Carolina, arriving on April 19. There, Davis learned that President Lincoln had been assassinated five days earlier—by Confederate sympathizer John Wilkes Booth. Moreover, new president Andrew Johnson had accused Davis of being part of the plot to kill Lincoln. Davis was now an outlaw; in two weeks Johnson would offer a $100,000 reward for his capture. While addressing a street crowd in Washington, Johnson said he would hang Davis and Confederate political leaders if he got the chance.

On April 26, General Johnston surrendered his army to General Sherman at Durham Station, North Carolina. Davis, though, was still on the run. Captain William H. Parker urged

After four years of civil war, an estimated 630,000 deaths and over 1 million wounded, General Robert E. Lee surrendered to Lieutenant General Ulysses S. Grant on April 9, 1865. Still, Davis stubbornly refused to give up, believing that he could reorganize the government in Texas. This print from May 5, 1865, shows Davis fleeing Richmond after the defeat of the Confederacy.

him to leave the country, but Davis was repulsed by the suggestion. Noted officer Basil Duke, as recounted in *Jefferson Davis: Confederate President*: "He seemed to cling obstinately to the hope of continuing the struggle in order to accomplish the great end of Southern independence—his whole soul was given to that thought…."

With other officials, Davis journeyed into South Carolina and then into Georgia. On May 5, Davis and remaining officials held their last meeting, and the Confederate government was finally dissolved. Davis, though, continued to flee, and the next day he hooked up with his family. But on May 9, while making camp near a creek in Irwinville, Georgia, the fugitive Davis family spent their last night together.

The next morning, Davis stepped out of his tent after hastily throwing on his wife's raincoat. Soon, it was obvious that the area was teeming with Union cavalrymen, and Corporal George Munger nabbed the famous fugitive. After defying the United States government for four years and three months, Davis finally knew that the fight was over. "God's will be done," he said.

9

Prisoner
and Legend

Upon capture on May 10, 1865, Jefferson Davis and his family were taken to Macon, Georgia. Union officials showed no mercy as they sang a verse from "John Brown's Body": "We'll hang Jeff Davis from a sour apple tree." Troops then took the family by train to Augusta, Georgia, where they were transferred to a steamer. They journeyed down the Savannah River and then up the Atlantic coast, finally dropping anchor next to Fort Monroe, Virginia, on May 22. Jefferson was going to prison.

Unsure when (or if) he would ever see them again, Davis kissed his wife and children good-bye. He told Varina not to cry, for the sake of the kids. Even at this shattering moment, the appearance of self-control was important to him.

Officials led Davis to a dungeonlike cell. The only sunlight came through a small, barred window that overlooked

After his capture on May 10, 1865, Davis was held as a prisoner in Fort Monroe, Virginia (*above*). During the war, although Virginia became part of the Confederate States of America, Fort Monroe remained in Union hands. Charged with treason, Davis was detained here for two years until prominent citizens of both the North and the South posted his bail.

a moat. General Nelson Miles ordered that Davis be shackled in leg irons. When an officer and blacksmith arrived with the dreaded contraption, Davis finally lost his composure. He demanded and pleaded with the officer not to shackle him, but to no avail. As recounted in *The Prison Life of Jefferson Davis,* he became nearly hysterical, gasping for breath and crying, "Kill me, kill me, rather than inflict on me, and on my people through me, this insult worse than death."

MERCY FOR DAVIS

Immediately after the war, few people had expressed sympathy for Davis, even in the South. Many had considered him an unwavering dictator who had made wrong decisions and had let the war drag on too long. The Civil War had been a four-year nightmare. More than 140,000 Union and 70,000 Confederate troops had been killed, and total war-related deaths exceeded 600,000. Hundreds of thousands would carry war wounds the rest of their lives. The South's industries, plantations, and farms were in ruins. Several million freed slaves had no land or jobs. The difficult period of Reconstruction, in which the federal government would rebuild the South largely on its own terms, would last for 12 years. Some Southerners, fairly or not, largely blamed Davis for leading them down the hellish path.

But when news broke that Davis lay shackled in a dungeon, many people—in the North and the South—pleaded for mercy. On May 28, 1865, Secretary of War Edward M. Stanton ordered that the chains be removed. Nevertheless, conditions in the cell were miserable. It was damp, poorly ventilated, and brightly lit twenty-four hours a day. Davis was not allowed visitors, books (except the Bible), or even utensils, for fear that he might try to kill himself. He was so lonely that he befriended a mouse, feeding it crumbs from his daily bread. How far this man had fallen....

Beginning in August 1865, Davis was able to write letters to Varina, who lived freely in Georgia but was not allowed to leave the state. The children were sent to live with her mother in Canada. Varina remained passionately loyal to her husband. "My dear Husband, Husband, dear Saintly Husband," she wrote on November 7, 1865, "if I were to give reins to my pen, surged on by my quivering, longing heart, what might the indifferent eyes which first peruse these whilom sacred confidences, see to."

Varina heard that her husband's health was failing, and she began to fight on his behalf. She pressed for more humane treatment for him and campaigned for his release. At one point, she even met with Andrew Johnson. The president said he would consider pardoning Davis, but Davis would refuse

to apply for a pardon. To do so, he stated, would be a confession of guilt.

On May 3, 1866, Varina was allowed to visit Davis for the first time. She would write in her memoir that she was shocked by his "shrunken form and glassy eyes" and cheekbones that "stood out like those of a skeleton." Varina wrote that "his bed was so infested with insects as to give a perceptible odor to the room."

A FREE MAN

Back in 1865, federal authorities had discussed charging Davis with treason for his alleged connection to the Lincoln assassination. After finding no links between Davis and the murder, the government decided that any treason trial would have to be held in a civil court or in a state court in Virginia. However, judges felt they had no authority over Davis's case because he was being held by the military. Thus, in May 1867, military authorities brought Davis to Richmond, where he was to be transferred to the authority of the federal courts.

John C. Underwood, circuit court judge for the District of Virginia, ruled that Davis would be temporarily freed if his backers posted $100,000 in bail. Ten Richmond businessmen and several others posted the bail money. One of them was famed New York journalist Horace Greeley, who wanted the Davis problem to be solved in order to speed the country's healing process. In mid-May, Davis was released on bail.

Davis's court case would drag on for two years, and he wouldn't even have to appear in court until November 26, 1867. In the meantime, he enjoyed his freedom. Jefferson, Varina, and their son Willie traveled to New York City, then went to Montreal where they embraced their remaining children, Margaret and Jefferson. The Davises lived in Canada for a year, with anonymous donors paying the rent on their house. This troubled the proud family patriarch, who wished to support his family on his own. But as a foreigner in poor health, he could not find work in Canada.

In November 1867, Davis returned to Richmond, where he met his old friend Robert E. Lee. The ex-general would write to his wife that Davis "looks astonishingly well and is quite cheerful." Good news came on the 26th, when the trial was postponed until March because Chief Justice Salmon P. Chase failed to show up. In fact, this would be Davis's last appearance in court on this matter, for the government would never put together a case against him.

With Davis still in poor health, his doctor advised that he spend time recuperating in Europe. In July 1868, Jefferson and his family sailed to Liverpool, England. Over the next year, he explored England, Wales, France, and Scotland. He made the acquaintance of dukes and earls, and he hooked up with Confederate friends who had moved to Great Britain.

ILLS AND SORROW

In the fall of 1869, Davis finally found a job. The Carolina Life Insurance Company of Memphis asked him to be president of its company. Leaving his family in London temporarily, Jefferson settled in to his new position. He would finally be able to support his family on his own, but unfortunately more misery followed. He struggled to drum up business due to a troubled economy, and he used much of his salary to pay off personal debts. Moreover, Varina was in ill health.

In September 1870, Davis returned to England to bring his family back to Baltimore, where he kept his offices. But more bad news followed. Jefferson's older brother, Joseph, died on September 18, and Robert E. Lee passed away on October 12. "He was my friend," Davis stated, as told in *Jefferson Davis: The Man and His Hour*, "and in that word is included all that I could say of any man."

Davis, who had survived so much suffering and death, saw much more of it. Varina suffered from anxiety and depression, and in October 1872, their ten-year-old son Willie battled diphtheria. When Davis came home from a business trip, his son was about to die. "I thought of the bright boy I had left at home, the hope and pride of my house," he mourned days after Willie's death, as recounted in Varina's memoir. "I have had more than the ordinary allotment of disappointment and sorrow."

And more followed in 1873. Varina's health did not improve. Daughter Maggie became seriously ill. Davis's sister Lucinda died. He resigned from the troubled Carolina Life Insurance Company. To top off the horrible year, Jefferson battled fever that fall, and at several points he wondered if he was going to survive. After getting better, he relapsed.

A GREAT PLACE TO WRITE A BOOK

Despite their many troubles, Jefferson and Varina endured. And as hard as it is to imagine, Davis found contentment in his later years. In the mid-1870s, he became increasingly popular in the South. He spoke at fairs and to veterans groups through-out the South, always receiving thunderous applause. Support-ers urged him to run for U.S. senator, representing Mississippi. But Davis was not even an American citizen, for he refused to take an oath of allegiance to the United States.

In 1877, Davis found a publisher who supported a book that he wanted to write. Over the next three years, Jefferson—working with former Confederate officer W.T. Walthall—wrote about the rise and fall of the Confederacy. Davis found a wonderful place to live, thanks largely to a widow named Sara Dorsey. A great admirer of Davis, Dorsey set him up in a cottage on her Mississippi estate, situated on the Gulf of Mexico. For Davis, the estate, called Beauvoir, was pure heaven. As he wrote his book, he could hear the waves splashing on the nearby beach. "The soft air, here, is delicious," he wrote in one of his letters. An orange grove and

At the invitation of novelist Sara Dorsey, Davis moved into Beauvoir to write his memoirs. Varina later joined him. In 1998, Beauvoir became the home of the Jefferson Davis Presidential Library and Museum. In 2005, the main residence, along with other buildings on the estate, was severely damaged by Hurricane Katrina. In 2008, restoration efforts were completed and the house reopened on the 200th anniversary of Davis's birth.

magnolia trees surrounded the house, and often he rode his horse through a nearby forest.

For several reasons, including an intense jealousy of Sara Dorsey, Varina refused to move to Beauvoir to be with her husband. But in the summer of 1878, she relented—and was glad she did. Varina enjoyed taking dictation from her husband, and she smiled when he sang during his work. But happiness never lasted long with this star-crossed couple. In October 1878, they suffered another tragedy: Jefferson Jr. died of yellow fever. Thus, for the fourth time, the couple buried a child. Though both of their daughters remained, all four of their sons were gone. The emotional toll of Jeff Jr.'s death affected his parents' physical health. Dorsey, ironically, cared for Varina—the woman who had once despised her.

But the Davis couple seemed to outlast all. Dorsey died on July 4, 1879. Out of devotion to her former president, she willed to Davis all of her property, which included Beauvoir and three small plantations. Davis was happy to have his own home, and he welcomed friends and admirers who came to visit. After lapsing well behind schedule on his memoir, Davis finally finished the two-volume book in April 1881. It was titled *The Rise and Fall of the Confederate Government.* However, few readers had the patience to read all 1,561 (often rambling) pages. Critics panned the book, and sales were low.

From 1882 to 1888, Davis enjoyed his twilight years. He and Varina remained at Beauvoir, and he spent time with his grandchildren. He also traveled and spoke throughout the South, always to warm receptions. In 1888, he agreed to begin work on another book, *A Short History of the Confederate States of America,* which he finished in October of that year.

HIS FINAL DAYS

Ironically, the man who had survived two wars, imprisonment, severe illnesses, and repeated personal tragedies lost his life due to a chilly rain. While en route to Brierfield in November 1888, Davis got stuck in a wintery storm in New Orleans. He made it to Brierfield, but after he developed bronchitis, Varina had him transported back to New Orleans. An ambulance took him to a friend's house, where Varina tended to him for three weeks.

As he lay on his deathbed, Davis told Varina not to tell his daughters about his illness, saying he might get better. Thus, even while dying he stayed true to character: refusing to show

Two months after completing *A Short History of the Confederate States of America*, in October 1889, Davis died in New Orleans at the age of 81. His funeral was one of the largest seen in the South. He has received many posthumous honors, including the removal by Congress in 1978 of the ban on Davis accusing him of violating Section 3 of the 14th Amendment. This amendment bars from office anyone that violates the oath to protect the Constitution by serving in the Confederacy.

his vulnerability and refusing to admit defeat. On December 6, 1889, at age 81, Jefferson Davis passed away.

Eleven years after Reconstruction, Southern pride surged throughout the Cotton Belt in 1889. In New Orleans, great throngs paid their respects to Davis in the largest funeral that the South had ever held. Six black horses pulled a carriage that carried the casket, which was draped with a Confederate flag. Multiple bands and thousands of Confederate soldiers accompanied the funeral procession.

After Davis's death, Varina showed her eternal devotion by writing a loving memoir about her husband. She also wanted to move his remains from New Orleans to a permanent, more appropriate location. Kentucky and Mississippi vied to make their state the eternal resting place, but Varina decided on the capital of the Confederacy. In 1893, Davis's body was exhumed in New Orleans and buried in Hollywood Cemetery in Richmond, Virginia. Varina, upon her death in 1906, was buried there, too, as were all six of the couple's children. Only in death were all eight members of the Davis family ever together.

THE LEGEND OF JEFFERSON DAVIS

Jefferson Davis ranks among the most controversial political figures in American history. Many see him as the man who started the Civil War. Although he initially rejected secession (for fear of war), he did eventually support it—even before he became president of the Confederacy. He also ordered the attack on Fort Sumter, sparking the war. And once the war began, he insisted on fighting to the bitter end, even though the war's final months brought only death and destruction to the South.

As commander in chief, Davis was accused of cronyism (putting his friends in high positions) and autocratic rule (a reflection of his military training). He stayed out of the spotlight throughout his presidency, making Confederate citizens suspicious of their leader. Some of his strategic decisions worked out well, while others led to disaster. Many wonder why Davis entered the war in the first place, considering the Union was far more populated and powerful. To this day,

WINNIE DAVIS: DAUGHTER OF THE CONFEDERACY

Jefferson Davis's youngest child, Varina Anne, named after her mother, was born in the Confederate White House in 1864. Her father nicknamed her "Winnie." In 1886, while accompanying her father to Atlanta for a monument dedication, she gained her other nickname: "Daughter of the Confederacy."

When Winnie was 15 years old, her parents sent her to Germany to further her education. Several years later, when she returned to the United States, she lived with her parents at their Beauvoir estate outside of Biloxi, Mississippi.

Winnie accompanied her father to reunions of Confederate organizations throughout the South, and she became a favorite of the many veterans. After her father's death in 1889, she moved to New York City with her mother to pursue a literary career. She wrote several books, including *An Irish Knight of the Nineteenth Century* and *A Romance of Summer Seas*.

While in Rhode Island for the "social season," she contracted malarial gastritis, and she died in September 1898. Winnie was so loved throughout the South that she was buried with full military honors in the Hollywood Cemetery in Richmond. A mourning angel marks her resting place.

many black and white Americans despise Davis because of his unyielding allegiance to slavery.

Yet through much of the South, Davis has been hailed as a hero. Supporters point to his humane treatment of his slaves and to his personal kindness and loving nature. They recall his deep knowledge of military history, his love of the South, and his inspirational orations. They recount his bravery in the field of battle and, most of all, his courage to stand up to the North—which many believe had tried to impose its will on the South. He was David (or Davis!) versus Goliath, the noble underdog who took a stand and fought to the finish.

Throughout the South, and even in Washington, D.C., monuments and statues have been dedicated to the Confederate president. In Mississippi, Georgia, and Texas, counties have been named after him. Mississippi and Alabama celebrate Davis's birthday every June, and in Florida, his birthday is a legal and public holiday.

The South will never forget Jefferson Finis Davis, the first—and last—president of the Confederate States of America.

CHRONOLOGY

1808   Jefferson Finis Davis born June 3 in Kentucky to Samuel and Jane Davis.

1824   Enters the U.S. Military Academy in September.

1828   Begins service in the U.S. Army in October.

1835   Marries Sarah Taylor on June 17; she dies three months later of malaria on September 15.

1836   Settles into a quiet life as a cotton planter on his Brierfield plantation in Mississippi.

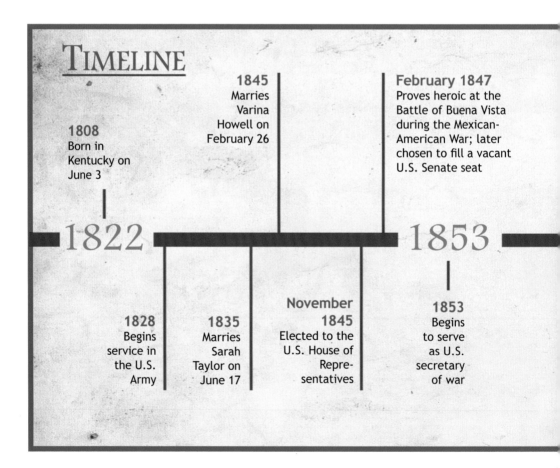

TIMELINE

1808
Born in Kentucky on June 3

1845
Marries Varina Howell on February 26

February 1847
Proves heroic at the Battle of Buena Vista during the Mexican-American War; later chosen to fill a vacant U.S. Senate seat

1822 — 1853

1828
Begins service in the U.S. Army

1835
Marries Sarah Taylor on June 17

November 1845
Elected to the U.S. House of Representatives

1853
Begins to serve as U.S. secretary of war

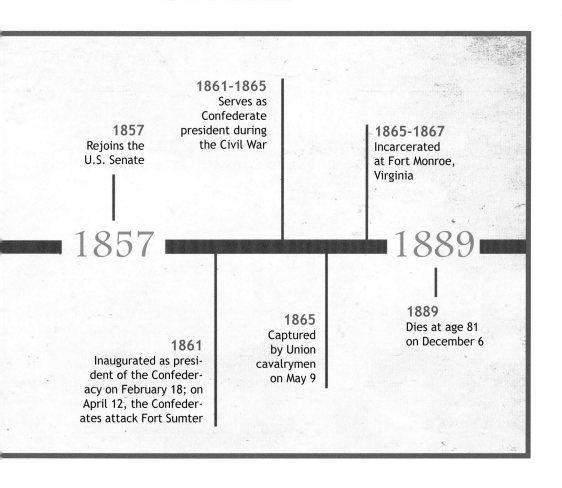

1845 Marries Varina Howell on February 26; in November, Davis is elected by Mississippians to the U.S. House of Representatives.

1847 Leads an impressive victory at the Battle of Buena Vista during the Mexican-American War, despite getting shot in the foot.

Chosen by the Mississippi legislature to fill a vacant U.S. Senate seat in December.

1853 Begins a productive four-year term as U.S. secretary of war.

1854 His son Samuel dies on June 30; all four of his sons will die in his lifetime.

1857
Rejoins the
U.S. Senate

1861-1865
Serves as
Confederate
president during
the Civil War

1865-1867
Incarcerated
at Fort Monroe,
Virginia

1857

1889

1861
Inaugurated as president of the Confederacy on February 18; on April 12, the Confederates attack Fort Sumter

1865
Captured
by Union
cavalrymen
on May 9

1889
Dies at age 81
on December 6

1857 Rejoins the U.S. Senate.

1861 Delivers his farewell address on January 21 after withdrawing from the Senate.

Inaugurated as president of the Confederate States of America on February 18.

On Davis's orders, the Confederates attack Fort Sumter on April 12, triggering the Civil War.

On May 29, Davis arrives at his new home in Richmond, Virginia, the new capital of the Confederacy.

1862 Assigns General Robert E. Lee to command the Army of Northern Virginia; tours the war's western theater to review the Confederate armies.

1864 **Fall** Tries to rally support for the Confederacy during a trip to Georgia.

1865 Flees Richmond on April 3 as Union troops descend upon the city.

1865 Captured by Union cavalrymen in Irwinville, Georgia, on May 9.

1865-1867 Incarcerated at Fort Monroe, Virginia.

1869 Becomes president of the Carolina Life Insurance Company in Memphis, Tennessee.

1881 Completes his memoir, *The Rise and Fall of the Confederate Government.*

1889 Dies at age 81 on December 6. His funeral will be the grandest ever held in the South.

GLOSSARY

abolitionist   A person who supported the end of slavery.

annexation   The addition of territory to an existing country or state.

aristocrats   Wealthy, typically well-educated people who occupy a high, powerful place in society.

armory   A place where the military stores its weapons and ammunition.

artillery   A large piece of military equipment.

blockade   A wartime tactic that is meant to isolate an area of importance to the enemy, such as a port.

cabinet   A body of high-ranking members of government, usually within the executive branch.

cadet   An officer-in-training at a military academy.

Confederate States of America (Confederacy)   The Southern states that seceded from the United States in 1861.

delegate   A representative of a state or organization who is authorized to act on its behalf.

demerit   A mark against a student for misconduct or failure.

diplomatic relations   Negotiations between nations.

dissolution   The end of existence.

enlist   Join the military.

expansionists   Those who wanted the United States to expand its territory.

fugitive   Someone who is trying to elude justice and whom law officers are trying to apprehend.

imports   Goods brought in to one's country.

inauguration   The ceremonial induction into a position.

legislature   A group of elected officials who create laws.

memoir   An author's account of his or her experiences.

militia   A group of citizens organized for military service.

munitions   Weapons and ammunition.

pardon   A formal act of liberating someone.

plantation   A farm or estate where cash crops are grown on a large scale.

provisional   Under terms not yet fully worked out or agreed upon; temporary.

regiment   A military unit consisting of smaller units. A typical regiment during the Civil War included more than 1,000 troops.

retreat   A withdrawal of troops to a more favorable position.

secede   Withdraw from the union.

sovereignty   The ultimate authority within territorial boundaries.

statesman   A respected leader in international or national affairs.

tariff   A tax on imported goods.

treason   The betrayal of one's own country.

Union   The United States, particularly during the Civil War.

BIBLIOGRAPHY

BOOKS

Alfriend, Frank H. *The Life of Jefferson Davis.* Cincinnati and Chicago: Caxton Publishing House, 1868.

Arnold, James R. *Divided in Two: The Road to Civil War.* Breckenridge, Colo.: Twenty-First Century Books, 2001.

Belanger, Jeff. *Ghosts of War: Restless Spirits of Soldiers, Spies, and Saboteurs.* Hawthorne, N.J.: Career Press, 2006.

Burke, Davis. *The Long Surrender.* New York: Random House, 1985.

Canfield, Cass. *The Iron Will of Jefferson Davis.* New York: Harcourt Brace Jovanovich, 1978.

Cooper, Jr., William J. *Jefferson Davis: American.* New York: Alfred A. Knopf, 2000.

Craven, John Joseph. *Prison Life of Jefferson Davis.* New York: G. W. Dillingham, 1905.

Davis, Jefferson. *Private Letters: 1823–1889.* New York: Harcourt, Brace & World, Inc., 1966.

Davis, Varina. *Jefferson Davis, Ex-President of the Confederate States of America.* New York: Belford Company, 1890.

———. *Jefferson Davis, Ex-President of the Confederate States of America Part One V2: A Memoir by His Wife.* Whitefish, Mont.: Kessinger Publishing, 2006.

Davis, William C., consultant. *The Civil War Chronicle.* Lincolnwood, Ill.: Publications International, Ltd., 2004.

———. *Jefferson Davis: The Man and His Hour.* New York: HarperCollins, 1991.

Eaton, Clement. *Jefferson Davis.* New York: The Free Press, 1977.

Eicher, David J. *The Longest Night: A Military History of the Civil War.* New York: Simon and Schuster, 2001.

Gallagher, Gary W., et al. *The American Civil War: The Mighty Scourge of War.* London: Osprey Publishing, 2003.

Hattaway, Herman and Richard E. Beringer. *Jefferson Davis, Confederate President.* Lawrence: University of Kansas Press, 2002.

Hattaway, Herman, and Archer Jones. *How the North Won: A Military History of the Civil War.* Champaign: University of Illinois Press, 1991.

Howard, Blair. *Battlefields of the Civil War: A Guide for Travellers, Volume 2.* Winston-Salem, N.C.: Hunter Publishing, 1995.

Jones, Wilmer L. *Generals in Blue and Gray.* Mechanicsburg, Penn.: Stackpole Books, 2006.

Jordan, Robert Paul. *The Civil War.* Washington, D.C.: National Geographic Society, 1969.

Lincoln, Abraham and Charles M. Segal. *Conversations with Lincoln.* Piscataway, N.J.: Transaction Publishers, 2002.

Long, Barbara. *The Civil War Day by Day: An Almanac, 1861–1865.* Cambridge, Mass.: Da Capo Press, 1985.

McElroy, Robert McNutt. *Jefferson Davis: The Unreal and the Real.* The Robert M. McElroy Papers, Kraus Reprint Co., 1969.

McPherson, James M. *Battle Cry of Freedom: The Civil War Era.* New York: Oxford University Press, 2003.

Meyers, Donald J. *And the War Came: The Slavery Quarrel and the American Civil War.* New York: Algora Publishing, 2005.

Shaff, Morris: *Jefferson Davis: His Life and Personality.* Boston: John W. Luce and Company, 1922.

Smith, Jean Edward. *Grant.* New York: Simon and Schuster, 2001.

Stevens, John Austin, et al. *Magazine of American History with Notes and Queries.* New York: A. S. Barnes, 1886.

Strode, Hudson. *Jefferson Davis: American Patriot.* New York: Harcourt, Brace and Company, 1955.

Tate, Allen. *Jefferson Davis: His Rise and Fall, A Biographic Narrative.* Whitefish, Mont.: Kessinger Publishing, 2006.

WEB SITES

Civil War Preservation Trust
http://www.civilwar.org

Fordham University
http://www.fordham.edu

Furman University
http://facweb.furman.edu

The National Archives
http://www.archives.gov

The Papers of Jefferson Davis
http://jeffersondavis.rice.edu

Time Magazine
http://www.time.com

The University of Tennessee
http://sunsite.utk.edu

⚔ FURTHER RESOURCES ⚔

Burch, Joann J. *Jefferson Davis: President of the Confederacy.* Springfield, N.J.: Enslow Publishers, 1998.

Cartmell, Donald. *Civil War 101: Everything You Ever Wanted to Know About the North, the South, the Leaders, the Battles, and the History.* New York: Gramercy Books, 2004.

Collins, Donald E. *The Death and Resurrection of Jefferson Davis.* Lanham, M.D.: Rowman & Littlefield Publishers, 2005.

Cooper, William J. *Jefferson Davis: The Essential Writings.* New York: Modern Library, 2004.

Dickson, Keith D. *The Civil War for Dummies.* Hoboken, N.J.: Wiley Publishing, 2001.

Griffin, John Chandler. *A Pictorial History of the Confederacy.* Jefferson, N.C.: McFarland & Company, 2004.

Hyslop, Steve. *Eyewitness to the Civil War.* Washington, D.C.: National Geographic, 2006.

Kelly, C. Brian. *Best Little Stories from the Civil War, with Varina: Forgotten First Lady.* Nashville: Cumberland House Publishing, 1998.

King, Perry Scott. *Jefferson Davis.* New York: Chelsea House, 1990.

Kinney Williams, Jean. *Jefferson Davis: President of the Confederate States of America.* Minneapolis: Compass Point Books, 2005.

Schneider, Dorothy. *An Eyewitness History of Slavery in America: From Colonial Times to the Civil War.* New York: Checkmark Books, 2001.

Wisler, G. Clifton. *When Johnny Went Marching: Young Americans Fight the Civil War.* New York: HarperCollins, 2001.

WEB SITES

Beauvoir: The Jefferson Davis Home and Presidential Library
http://www.beauvoir.org

CivilWar.com
http://www.civilwar.com

The Civil War Home Page
http://www.civil-war.net

Jefferson Davis
http://www.civilwarhome.com/jdavisbio.htm

Jefferson Davis
http://www.jeffersondavis.net/

PICTURE CREDITS

PAGE

INDEX

 ABOUT THE AUTHOR

DAVID ARETHA has authored more than 30 books for young readers and has edited dozens of books, specializing in history. His editing credits include *The Blue and the Gray, Civil Rights Chronicle,* and *World War II Chronicle.*